Teaching with Comics and Graphic Novels

This text will allow you to harness students' love of comics and graphic novels while increasing critical thinking and engagement in the classroom. Author Tim Smyth offers a wide variety of lessons and ideas for using comics to teach close reading, working with textual evidence, literature adaptations, symbolism and culture, sequencing, essay writing, and more. He also models how to use comics to tackle tough topics and enhance social-emotional learning. Throughout the book, you'll find a multitude of practical resources, including a variety of lesson plans—some quick and easy activities as well as more detailed ready-to-use unit plans. These thoughtful lessons meet the Common Core State Standards and are easy to adapt for any subject area or grade level to fit into your curriculum. Add this book to your professional library, and you'll have a new and exciting way of reaching and teaching your students!

Tim Smyth is a high school social studies educator and Reading Specialist of more than 20 years who travels the country giving professional development to educators on the power of teaching with comics. Smyth was also part of a global online comics in education program through the US State Department. He has been published in many outlets, such as PBS, and he also shares many resources on his website, TeachingWithComics.com. Smyth loves interacting on social media (@historycomics) and is the founder of two Facebook education communities—"Comic Book Teachers" and "Teaching With Comics". He lives in Bucks County, Pennsylvania with his wife and three comic book-loving children.

Also Available from Routledge
Eye On Education
www.routledge.com/k-12

Passionate Readers:
The Art of Reaching and Engaging Every Child
Pernille Ripp

Passionate Learners, 2e:
How to Engage and Empower Your Students
Pernille Ripp

Identity-Affirming Classrooms:
Spaces that Center Humanity
Erica Buchanan-Rivera

What to Look for in Literacy:
A Leader's Guide to
High-Quality Instruction
Angela Peery and Tracey Shiel

Authentic Assessment in Social Studies:
A Guide to Keeping it Real
David Sherrin

The Flexible ELA Classroom:
Practical Tools for Differentiated Instruction in Grades 4–8
Amber Chandler

The Writing Workshop Teacher's Guide to
Multimodal Composition (6–12)
Angela Stockman

Teaching with Comics and Graphic Novels

Fun and Engaging Strategies to Improve Close Reading and Critical Thinking in Every Classroom

Tim Smyth

Routledge
Taylor & Francis Group

NEW YORK AND LONDON

Cover image: © Getty Images

First published 2023
by Routledge
605 Third Avenue, New York, NY 10158

and by Routledge
4 Park Square, Milton Park, Abingdon, Oxon, OX14 4RN

Routledge is an imprint of the Taylor & Francis Group, an informa business

© 2023 Tim Smyth

The right of Tim Smyth to be identified as author of this work has been asserted in accordance with sections 77 and 78 of the Copyright, Designs and Patents Act 1988.

Library of Congress Cataloging-in-Publication Data
A catalog record for this book has been requested

ISBN: 978-1-032-27177-4 (hbk)
ISBN: 978-0-367-52037-3 (pbk)
ISBN: 978-1-003-29167-1 (ebk)

DOI: 10.4324/9781003291671

Typeset in Palatino
by Apex CoVantage, LLC

Dedication

For Charlotte, Liam, and Teagan—you are why I do what I do
For Joan—my friend, my wife, my muse, my everything

Contents

Acknowledgements

None of my educational journey would have happened without the loving support and inspiration of my family. My wife, Joan, is the most dedicated and supportive educator I have ever met, and she made me want to be a teacher like her—integrating love, creativity, and humanity, while having high expectations and believing in students. My three kids, Charlotte, Liam, and Teagan, are always giving me ideas on integrating comics as we share a love of all things reading. My family is often in the audience during my presentations as they willingly travel the country with me and keep my anxieties at bay with their support. I have even been lucky enough to have them present on panels with me! I would never have the courage to do what I do without them always cheering me on. I also have to thank my biggest fan, Terrie, the most wonderful mother-in-law and educator. She was the one who had me present for my first school in-services and literacy nights.

Of course, I could not be sharing lessons and ideas with you unless I had curious and inspiring students who are always willing to be a part of this collaborative journey. I can't tell you how many times students have helped me see the world in a different way, shaped my lessons, and kept me revising lessons. We have laughed and cried together, learned from each other, and they give hope for the future of our world.

AJ Juliani helped me overcome my self-doubt and see value in sharing what was happening in my classroom. He encouraged me to join social media, create a blog, and share what my students and I were doing. I initially thought that this would be "showing-off" and, really, that few would show interest outside of my students. Matt Heppe, a much-respected teacher colleague also joined with AJ in encouraging me to share. Through their encouragement, I began a blog and joined social media, and I never looked back. Not only have I been able to share with other educators, but I have also learned so much from teachers around the world. I am forever thankful for my social media family, and I highly encourage you to share your educational journey as well. We need to help inspire the next generation of teachers and to let the world know how amazing it is to be in education.

After braving the social media waters, I had a really tough year in teaching and seriously considered leaving the profession. However, Vicky Pasquantonio from PBS NewsHour Extra reached out to me and asked if I wanted to write an article about teaching with comics. Of course I said yes and was immediately rewarded with love from educators and fellow nerds from around the world. If it had not been for AJ, Matt, and Vicky, if I had not gotten over my fears to share my journey, I might very well not be a teacher today.

I am thankful to my Gwynedd Mercy University family, professors, and administrators, who have shown me such great support in my teaching with comics journey. My open-minded professors gave me much encouragement as I wrote my paper on the integration of comics as literature in the classroom. I was initially hesitant to share this topic idea with them, but they responded with their own curiosity about the topic. Years later, I continue to be a part of the Gwynedd family, being a member of the alumni board and being asked to come back to guest lecture.

Without Lauren Davis, my editor from Routledge, taking a chance on me, this book would have been left as a "what if" on my bucket list. My family and I will be forever thankful for her kindness, encouragement, patience, and feedback in making this book possible.

Meet the Author

Tim Smyth, MS Reading Specialist, has been teaching social studies for over 20 years at Wissahickon High School in Ambler, Pennsylvania and has also served as chair for his social studies department. Tim has presented about how he uses comics and pop culture in his classroom at numerous conferences across the United States, including comic book conventions and national educational and library conferences. He has also guest lectured at multiple universities and gives school district–level professional development on comics as engaging literature. Additionally, he also writes curriculum and teacher guides for multiple publishers, including PBS, MacMillan, and Scholastic. Tim has also served as an online educator and consultant for the US State Department in a global online comics program.

Tim maintains a comprehensive website and blog on all things comics in education at www.TeachingWithComics.com. You can find Tim on social media @Historycomics, email him Historycomicsguy@gmail.com, and join the ongoing collaborative discussions on his two Facebook pages—"Teaching With Comics" and "Comic Book Teachers". Feel free to reach out with questions or to bring him out to your event.

Preface

Comics = Literacy

Comics = Literacy as they serve as the perfect tool for creating dynamic readers, writers, artists, and deep thinkers in your classes. More than that, comics inspire students to dream and to become heroes themselves.

I am a teacher. Whenever I attend a professional development session in my district, at an EdCamp, state or national education conference, and YES—at a comic book convention, I always want to walk away with something I can use in my class the next day. That is the intention of this book—to give you ideas that can be carried out in your class the very next day. In this book, I will not use overwhelming edu-speak that will lose you in needless jargon, but I will provide personal experiences from both my classroom and with my own children. I will tie lessons into Common Core standards and show you why comics are valuable learning tools. I wrote my master's paper as a Reading Specialist on using comics and pop culture to engage and help create critical readers and writers. Most of what you find here will be actual lessons that have been used to great effect in my classroom and with my own children to foster a love of reading and writing. I will be taking you on a personal journey that will give you a general understanding of comics and graphic novels and their use as tools of literacy in every classroom.

1

My Journey into Teaching with Comics

I Am a Teacher. I Am a Father.

I am a high school social studies teacher and MS Reading Specialist who gets to travel the USA giving professional development to educators on the importance of integrating comics in education. I get to work with the US State Department in a global online comics in education program, helping students find their voices and solve local and global issues. My workshops have been given at comic book conventions, state and national education conferences, school district in-services, libraries, universities, and even museums. I have been published by multiple outlets, such as PBS, on my educational journey and the connection to comics in education. I have worked with many comics publishers to develop teacher guides for comics. I bring with me a passion for what I do, and I love to encourage educators to embrace their passions and to integrate them into their classrooms. The purpose of this book is to give a general introduction to comics and graphic novels (these terms are used interchangeably as graphic novels are, at their core, just longer versions of a comic book), their positive impact on students of all ages, and specific lessons that can be used in classrooms across all grade levels and subject areas. I want to give you ideas that you can integrate into your classroom tomorrow. Specific lessons that I have used in my own teaching and that I know work well. I will not bog you down in needless edu-speak nor delve deeply into the theory of comics themselves. This is meant to be a collegial conversation amongst fellow educators, one that will continue well after reading this book.

DOI: 10.4324/9781003291671-1

After years of education experience, I understand what we as educators want, and this book will provide those in education with:

1. "Permission" to integrate their passions and instructions on how to find others who share this passion. I will share my experience of almost leaving teaching until I integrated my passion for comics into the classroom that ignited the enthusiasm of my students. I will share how to use social media to connect to like-minded educators.
2. Methods to defend the use of comics to administration, parents, and fellow teachers—including ties to **Common Core Standards.**
3. A basic introduction to comics, how to read them, and how to impart this to students.
4. Specific lesson plan ideas that can be tailored to multiple levels and disciplines—not a bunch of theory.
5. Titles of books to use in the classroom and how to get them with small budgets.
6. Ways to get kids interested in reading.
7. Ideas on how to bring something different, fun, and meaningful into the classroom.
8. Methods to encourage students to be makers of content and not just takers.
9. How to connect subject area topics to pop culture/modern society current with student culture to create a connection between the two.
10. How to create a culture of cross-curricular ideas and planning.
11. Answers to the common questions I get during my workshops— Where do I start? How do I get comics?

The overall goal of this book is to open the minds of educators to the use of comics as meaningful and engaging literature that help all levels of readers. Comics are societal artifacts, a break from the textbook, and a way to engage our 21st-century globally diverse society. Again, this will be reached by the sharing of my own personal experiences and successes in specific lessons and the offer to continue the conversation even after finishing the book.

My journey with comics as literacy really goes back to my childhood days of reading comics in my bedroom and getting lost in all the amazing stories. Superheroes resonate with all of us and are our modern mythology, much like those of the Greeks and Romans. When my bedroom door was shut, I became Batman, Spider-Man, Superman—these were heroes who were able to overcome difficult circumstances and still go on to save the world. The X-Men were outcasts from society, loners who were ridiculed, bullied, and often cut off from their families. Yet they were able to overcome their biological family issues by joining a new family who accepted them and showed them love. They were able to defend the earth from many monsters, including isolation. Growing up, I was also able to make a connection to my own hero, my father. I saw him as a superhero when I saw him put on his Philadelphia police uniform and go out each day to save the world. I heard stories of him rescuing people from burning buildings, saving children from horrible circumstances, and ridding the world of bad guys, and for me that brought comics to life. Even now, as an adult, comics still serve this purpose for me as I struggle with events in my childhood, my anxiety, and bouts of depression. I can still see myself in these heroes, and I know many others feel the same.

While my love for comics never waned, as a beginning teacher, these books were not included in my classroom lessons. I did not decorate my classroom with superhero posters, nor did I have any comic books in sight. This would make my current students laugh as my current classroom library overflows with comics, graphic novels, posters, and more. When I began my journey as a teacher, I felt as though I needed to prove myself as an academic and promptly filled my room with traditional resources and literature. I would not even have imagined using comics as I was trapped in the misconception that I currently rail against—comics are just for kids, they are just capes and tights, and they are not literature. However, my professional journey changed due to several fortuitous events culminating in a serious moment when I considered leaving teaching. However, it was the decision to fully integrate my passion for comics and Hip Hop into my teaching that literally saved me and made me, in a powerful sense, a new teacher all over again. I reexamined my content and resources and wondered how to change what I did to make the lessons more engaging, more cross-curricular, more skills-based, and more fun for the students and me. Now, I get to travel the country giving professional development on comics in education and get to share my ideas. Like many educators, I once thought I was "just a teacher"—I never thought that others would care much about what I did and thought sharing my ideas in a blog or through other means would just come off as bragging. Luckily, I had several people in my life who encouraged me to share through Twitter, Instagram, and blogging about my classroom experiences, and everything changed. I hope to encourage you to do the same because what we do in our classrooms is important. We need YOUR voice to help shape the conversation about what education truly is and inspire the next generation of educators.

My love for comics was unexpected, given the academic credibility I needed when I decided to obtain my Master's Degree as a Reading Specialist at Gwynedd Mercy University. I was the only male teacher in the program and one of only two secondary/content area teachers. Many expressed surprise that a high school social studies teacher would be undertaking a

Reading Specialist program as reading is generally thought to be a skill taught in elementary school or, at higher levels, more fit for Language Arts class. However, I firmly believe that all educators are teachers of reading and that analytical reading and writing are the utmost important skills. I believe that all classrooms need to have libraries and that we all need to model reading for our students, share what we read, and share HOW we read. In this university program, I was repeatedly shown studies that showed boys don't read as much as girls, nor do they read as deeply. Yet growing up, my public library card was my most prized possession, and I loved reading and simply could not personally identify with this educational research. According to these studies, it wasn't just that boys weren't reading, but males of all ages. I listened to some of the other elementary teachers in my program as they discussed similar issues in their classrooms of boys not reading. I began to ask questions, the most important being, what are you giving these boys to read? When some of the classroom titles were being shared by these teachers, an idea began to form in my head. I did not enjoy reading many of those titles in school either. I shuddered as I remembered reading *Anna Karenina* in high school. My English teacher was an amazing educator and did all he could to make the book come to life for us, but it just didn't click with me. As the weeks went on in his class, it really became a drag on my love of reading. Remembering this experience, I began to wonder if comics might be a possible answer. From my own personal experiences, I knew that there were meaningful stories, full of plot twists, mystery, high-level vocabulary, and so much in comics that perhaps others did not yet know about.

I brought my ideas to my professors at Gwynedd Mercy University. I was afraid of being scoffed at, but these open-minded professors found the idea to be as exciting as I did. I will be forever grateful as I began to excitedly research the efficacy of comic books in the classroom. There was not a lot of information to be had at the time, and I had to work hard to find that information. However, it was a true passion project, and I read anything I could find on the topic, drew on my personal experiences, and also tested the waters a bit in my own classroom. I wrote up an entire program about using comics and pop culture to increase classroom engagement in literacy. I really had a funny thought as I presented my findings and defended my paper to a room full of educators: The younger version of me was a large part of this presentation and was excitedly cheering me on, albeit in disbelief. My presentation began with how I used a paragraph from my social studies classroom textbook about the Battle of Thermopylae. I paired this description with images from the graphic novel *300* by Frank Miller, another sample from the textbook on the 100 Years War, and finally images from the comic *Crecy* by Warren Ellis. The end result of this experiment was that my students were able to learn so much more about this battle through the intersection of comics and the textbook. They were excited and engaged at using this new medium. I would never propose that comics can replace more traditional resources, but they are able to enhance our lessons.

While the premise of my Reading Specialist paper focused on using comics to engage boys, it quickly became so much more. I am not of the belief that there are certain books for boys and others for girls—there are just good stories. There are so many great female leads in comics and stories that are great for many interests. I have found the same success using comics with all of my students, regardless of gender. When we created the comic book club in my high school, the founding officers were three amazing young women, all with impressive encyclopedic knowledge of comics and pop culture. As will be shown throughout this book, comics have long reflected society and have become ever more inclusive of all peoples.

My three children also eventually became part of my ongoing research of engaging readers as they have a deep and meaningful love of all things reading. However, for my son, Liam, this was not always the case. He was labeled a "reluctant reader" in kindergarten by his teacher as he did not want to read the phonics books he was being given. Let's be honest, these books were unimaginative and left little chance to create excitement and engagement for any kid. As a family of readers who understand the critical importance of reading throughout life, his mother and I were obviously concerned. His teacher looked down on all things related to comics and thought his interest was interfering with his education. He began to act out a bit at school—even putting his hand out like Spider-Man and pretending to web his teacher at one point! He was already pigeon-holed as a struggling student and began to give up on school—I could see it happening before my eyes. I initially decided to double down and support the findings of this teacher and unfairly punished my son. I took away his superhero lunch box, school bag, and clothes. I told him he could earn them back by doing as his teacher said, by reading the books she wanted him to read. I now look back on this experience as something for which I will never be able to forgive myself as a parent or an educator. I should have known better as the evidence was clearly there to be seen. I thought of my own experience as a child and the research I had undertaken for my Reading Specialist degree. His teacher did not see any value in comics as literature, and her classroom was limited in both book options and decorations. My wife and I changed our approach with him, and I began to share my comics with Liam and buy him comics that were perfect for him. His love of reading, and confidence as a reader, almost immediately began to climb. We pulled all three of our kids out of this school as a result, and it was the right choice to make. My son now loves to read everything, not just comics. We need to keep this lesson in mind as parents and educators, just as I do in my classroom whenever possible. This is why I allow students to choose their own research topics, because I want them to be passionate about what they are researching—not just see learning through some assigned topic over which they will come to resent both me as a teacher and history as a discipline.

Despite my success in my graduate studies and with my own kids, a few years still passed before I really began to integrate comics into my class. It wasn't until I was discussing the new Spider-Man, Miles Morales, in my classroom as a current event that it all came together. Miles Morales has an African-American father and a Puerto Rican mother and was part of an intentional movement in comics to increase representation. I had one particular African-American student perk up at my discussion, and he stayed after class to discuss this new comic. This was a student with whom I did not have a strong connection in the classroom. He was a great student, but we had not connected on a personal level. However, we now had something in common to talk about, so I began bringing in my comics to show him, and our conversations began to grow. This young man was more impressed that Spider-Man looked like him than President Obama! As a teacher, we are forever grateful for moments like these when we can make connections with students, and it was then that I knew that I was onto something. I was able to share a personal passion of mine, and I began to get even more excited to come into the classroom every day. I began showcasing other comics as societal artifacts and explaining how they reflect the changing society around us. This is what makes comics such a powerful classroom resource as they are true societal mirrors. New comics come out every Wednesday, and what happens in our society is often reflected in these stories.

While I began to excitedly reimagine my approach to education, I finally had THAT year as a teacher. Events transpired that made me question everything I was as a teacher and my future in education. I went into a depression and found it hard to go to work, just wanting to stay in bed with the covers over my head. I spoke things over with my wife and began looking into options for another career. It's not that I no longer enjoyed teaching—I love being in the room with my students and count myself lucky to be in this profession. There were just too many outside things going on that were negatively impacting what was going on in my classroom. Then a real-life superhero came into my life, and I received a message from Vicky Pasquantonio, an editor from PBS Newshour. She had read my blog about connecting with students through comics and wanted to know if I would be interested in writing an article to be published by PBS. Of course, I took her up on the opportunity, and, when published, I immediately began receiving positive comments from people around the world. I took my family out to dinner to celebrate, and I cried tears of joy. This was a major turning point in my life as I found that my voice had value beyond my classroom and that what I was doing made an impact on people around the world. With this newfound encouragement, I decided to continue to share my ideas. I presented at my first comic book convention, even though I was absolutely terrified before getting on the stage. By the time it was over, I had people lined up to talk to me, to ask me questions, and to say thank you for what I was doing. My world opened up as I began to find my people. Again, I implore YOU to share your educational passion with the world and to inspire others while also gathering a support system of educators.

Additionally, I shared my article with my students, and they were so supportive in my efforts and even left amazing comments on my PBS article. I knew then, as I do now, that this journey was not solely my journey but all of ours. My students were able to see the value of an authentic audience, of following your passions, and of pushing beyond our comfort zones. So many students have told me that they admire the way I integrate my passions into the classroom and that it helps them to validate their own endeavors. Currently, we are experiencing teacher shortages across the country, fewer enrolled education majors in universities, and new teachers who leave the profession in the first few years. We need to inspire the next generation of teachers and those currently in the profession—and we do this by igniting our own passions and integrating our strengths. I have presented to education majors, and many often remark how great it is to hear that education is not all standardized tests and that creativity still has a place in the classroom. Administrators, please keep this in mind when planning your district's professional development days—encourage teachers to find ways to integrate their own personal passions into the classroom. Encourage them to share their journey with the world, to blog, to engage in Twitter chats, to create YouTube videos. We need to hear the voices of teachers and what is happening in their classrooms. As educators, we need to change and even drive the conversation.

Whenever I complete my presentations or workshops, I always have people come up to share with me how comics have had an impact in their lives. Many adults will tell me stories of how they learned to read through comics and are excited that they are now being used in classrooms. Many of us have that story of when a teacher took comics away from students—why? When we want students to read, why take away this obviously engaging medium? autistic adults, dyslexia, ADHD, and more have come to shake my hand to also tell me how comics enabled them to learn to read. Educators come and say thank you for giving them the permission they needed to bring their passion for comics into the classroom, that they were too hesitant to do so. One of my all-time favorite moments was when, following a guest lecture at Gwynedd Mercy University, a student came up to me and asked for my autograph. She had taken copious notes as I spoke and wanted me to sign them! It is these experiences that keep me going and have me traveling the country. I even befriended the PA Secretary of Education, Pedro Rivera, through social media, and he came to visit my classroom on the first day of school one year. Turns out that he also loves comics and understands the power they can bring to education. More than that, he always spoke about how teachers need to look for inspiration in each other. Teaching can often make educators feel as though they are on an island, but this can be dissipated when we share our successes, and failures, with one another.

2

Defense of Comics

Image 2.1 **Jarrett Lerner—vocabulary study**
Courtesy of Jarrett Lerner https://jarrettlerner.com/

DOI: 10.4324/9781003291671-2

Before sharing lesson plans and resources in the later chapters, I wanted to take a little bit of time to "defend" the use of comics in the classroom. There are still those who are not ready to accept comics as literature, although that number is dwindling fast. As such, it is important to be able to defend their use and how they can enhance the educational journey. There has been more and more research done on the use of comics, such as this wonderful study that I often cite and which Jarrett Lerner summed up in an inspiring illustration (see Image 2.1 Jarrett Lerner).

One major criticism that I hear is that comics are just for kids, and there is an assumption that the reading levels are just too low to be used in the classroom. I can tell you, from personal experience, that this is simply not the case. My kids have developed amazing vocabulary through comics. These are words that they have not heard in conversation or been exposed to in grade-level text. When I ask them about the word, they can absolutely explain to me the meaning, often understood through the natural built-in scaffolding that comics afford when image and text support one another. Comics are limited in how many words can be used in each panel, so the author and letterer must be selective in which text is included—this often necessitates using more complex words to get the idea across. In prose, the reader may either skip over these difficult words, try to make sense in context, or go and look up the word. These are all things that happen when reading a comic as well, but this medium has another advantage—images help make context. Readers of comics will develop close reading skills as they use the images to make sense of difficult vocabulary. One of my all-time favorite quotes that highlights this reality is a quote from Stan Lee himself. When asked about his word choice in comics, he answered, "I was determined to never talk down to the reader. I insisted on using college-level vocabulary. If a kid didn't know what a word meant, he'd get it by the use in the sentence by osmosis. If he had to go to a dictionary, that's not the worst thing in the world!"—**quote found** https://apnews.com/article/archive-21d1c51c9e774d84a58e33df453bba08 - Graphic Novels Foster Literacy, Staff Writer, December 9, 2017.

Many educators tell me that I really do have a comic for everything and are surprised at the depth and breadth of comic offerings on many topics beyond the traditional superheroes in capes and tights. Books, such as graphic memoirs, literary adaptations, and historical text certainly add to the legitimacy of comics as literature; however, we also must look at the superhero stories and understand their depth and reflection of us. Non–comic readers can have a certain prejudice against comics but are relatively easy to win over in conversation. I have opened many minds by explaining some of the literary and historical contexts of comics. For example, The Joker has his origins in *The Man Who Laughs* by Victor Hugo, and Stan Lee created Black Panther as he read reports about the actual organization. Some argue that Martin Luther King, Jr. and Malcolm X are reflected in the X-Men characters Charles Xavier and Magneto. The Hulk is heavily influenced by Frankenstein's Monster as well as Dr. Jekyll and Mr. Hyde. There are many such examples that exist throughout comics, and we can't forget that our literature is impacted by the events surrounding its creators.

As educators, we know it is best practice to make every attempt to reach our students where they are and to even adapt/personalize lessons whenever possible and appropriate. Comics are a wonderful resource to allow us to do just that, and I will share example lessons that showcase this inherent ability. Not only do comics empower students with various learning challenges, such as language learners, dyslexia, autism, reading delays, and more, they also allow all students to literally be seen in their classroom literature. However, there are some who overlook the power of comics as just gimmicks to engage the "reluctant reader" and to then move on to "real" books. In truth, comics bring learning to readers of all levels, including gifted and university-level students, and this will be discussed later in this book.

One of the most photographed parts of my presentations and school in-services is when I begin to cite Common Core and connections to comics. This often takes people by surprise, but Common Core standards are very supportive of the skills taught through comics. In fact, if you are not using comics in your classroom, you are not following Common Core. I firmly believe that all teachers, regardless of subject area, need to know the standards for reading and writing—this is not just the job of elementary and Language Arts teachers—we all play a part in our student's literacy. I will be using examples from the Pennsylvania standards as I implement them in my classroom, and they are very closely aligned with the national standards.

Here are some examples from the secondary standards:

Standard CC.8.6.H—

Draw evidence from informational texts to support analysis, reflection, and research. (There are so many wonderfully researched comics and graphic novels that students can use to support this standard. Often, authors share the process they undertook to create these comics.)

Standard CC.8.5.11–12.A

Cite specific textual evidence to support analysis of primary and secondary sources, connecting insights gained from specific details to an

understanding of the text as a whole. (This is the most important skill in a classroom—finding textual evidence. We do this through annotating Hip Hop lyrics, letters, poems, diary entries, political cartoons/propaganda, and comics. Visual and textual evidence support one another, and it is the visual evidence that is most open to debate and will challenge students to think much more deeply than traditional text. The following three standards will also support this idea.)

Standard—CC.8.5.11–12.C

Evaluate various explanations for actions or events and determine which explanation best accords with textual evidence, acknowledging where the text leaves matters uncertain.

Standard—CC.8.5.11–12.D

Determine the meaning of words and phrases as they are used in a text, including analyzing how an author uses and refines the meaning of a key term over the course of a text (e.g., how Madison defines faction in Federalist No. 10).

Standard—CC.8.5.11–12.E

Analyze in detail how a complex primary source is structured, including how key sentences, paragraphs, and larger portions of the text contribute to the whole.

Standard—8.1.W.C

Construct research on a historical topic using a thesis statement and demonstrate use of appropriate primary and secondary sources. (I allow my students to choose their own research paper topics—almost anything. Also, what teacher wants to read 150 papers on the causes of WWII? It can be daunting to choose any topic as students are often not used to this type of autonomy. Having a classroom full of comics can often spur research paper topics. A student is often drawn in by a cover and then reads the graphic novel/comic. This can be done in a much shorter time than reading a traditional book or going out onto the internet. Then more research with other sources will be undertaken.)

Following are some examples from the elementary standards:

◆ **Standard CC.1.1.K.B Demonstrate understanding of the organization and basic features of print. Follow words left to right, top to bottom, and page by page.** (Comics are an excellent vehicle to help students understand how the structure of print actually works. Not only are they immediately engaged, but they can use the pictures to help them find confidence in decoding this text. I'll even take it one step further as comics also teach 21st century reading skills in that the text does not always read in a linear fashion, much the way we read online.)

- **Standard CC.1.2.1.A Identify the main idea and retell key details of text.** (Comics help the student focus on the main idea, and the retelling is very powerful as students can draw their own summaries.)
- **CC.1.2.1.G Use the illustrations and details in a text to describe its key ideas.** (Yep!)
- **CC.1.2.4.G Interpret various presentations of information within a text or digital source and explain how the information contributes to an understanding of text in which it appears.**
- **CC.1.3.1.G Use illustrations and details in a story to describe characters, setting, or events.**
- **CC.1.3.5.G Analyze how visual and multimedia elements contribute to the meaning, tone, or beauty of a text (e.g., graphic novel, multimedia presentation of fiction, folktale, myth, poem).**
- **CC.1.4.K.M Use a combination of drawing, dictating, and writing to compose narratives that describe real or imagined experiences or events.**

The above are just a few standards that directly support using comics in the classroom, and I encourage you to look over your core standards again with this in mind. As you read through the rest of this book, also keep these standards in mind and how they would apply to your course and grade level.

I often share a short cheat sheet with educators when asked how to defend the importance of teaching with comics to administrators, parents, and fellow educators. Also, it is vital that we include students in our discussion of the how and why of our educational approaches.

21st Century Learning—as stated above, comics are similar in many ways to reading hypertext as a reader online will often not read in a linear fashion.

Close Reading/Annotating—comics force readers to slow down and look closely at the images. The images are an integral part of the story and add much value to it. Textual/visual evidence. The space between each panel in a comic is called a gutter. This is what really forces a comics reader to think deeply because so much takes place in this empty space. In a traditional text, the author specifically writes what is happening throughout the story. In this case, a reader doesn't have to use as much imagination as when reading a comic.

Common Core Skills

Not just a gimmick—using comics in the classroom is engaging, yes, but also skill-based.

Comics (sequential art) have been around for a long time. Think of the Bayeux Tapestry, stained-glass windows, Mexican Codex, the Egyptian Menna Tomb, and many more examples. More examples are cited in *Understanding Comics* by Scott McCloud.

Reading Olympics—my daughter is on the Reading Olympics team at her school, and my wife is a coach. My daughter told me that she had an advantage because many of the other students did not understand that the images in the graphic novels on the list added to the story. They had only read the text and missed much of the story.

Student Engagement—movies, TV shows, video games—encourage students to read the books that inspired these other mediums. Comics also help with reluctant or unconfident readers.

Inter-disciplinary—Comics easily create cross-curricular skillsets and ideas, including art.

Societal artifact / time capsule—comics come out every Wednesday and often portray the current society.

Representation—we all deserve to see ourselves in our heroes

Differentiation—comics can be used on all levels and are even being increasingly used in universities. I have used comics with emerging readers, students who are reading below grade level, non-native English speakers, Honors and Gifted students, and in Advanced Placement European History and AP Economics.

3

Resources

Now that you have a bit of background on the efficacy of comics in education and their importance in the classroom, how do you get them? Funding is always tight for educators, and we already spend a lot of our own money for our educational resources. I am always asked how I get the money to use these comics in my classroom. I am blessed to work in a district that supports this passion and has purchased class sets of the inspiring *March* Trilogy, based on Congressman John Lewis' life. We will discuss the use of this later on in the book, in Chapter 15. However, it is not realistic to ask for a class set of every comic that I want to use in the classroom, especially as I do not teach a comics class but integrate comics as part of my curriculum. As you can obviously guess, I am an avid comics reader and visit the comic book store every Wednesday, when new comics come out. Comics often serve as an insightful artifact into our society, and my mind is always racing when reading a comic as I think of ways to use it in the classroom. I want to buy so many and bring them into my classroom, but funds just don't allow this to happen. There are times, honestly, when I do spend my own money to buy a class set of a comic (such as Jim Zub's Champions comic—more on that later in chapter 9) as I know the immediate impact it will have on classroom discussions. However, there are other ways to integrate comics without having to buy a large number of them.

FREE online comics—There are actually many free online comics shared by authors, museums (like the Smithsonian), government

DOI: 10.4324/9781003291671-3

agencies (like the US State Department), and more. These
resources are absolutely free for use in an educational setting
and are easily accessed. Go to the free comics part of my website,
TeachingWithComics.com, where I keep an updated list of such
comics perfect for use in the classroom. I am always on the lookout
to add to this growing collection, so please feel free to reach out and
let me know what to add.

Free Comic Book Day—this is the first Saturday in May each year
(https://www.freecomicbookday.com/). This is such a perfect day
for literacy as comic book stores across the US open their doors
to everyone as they give away free comics! Keep in mind that not
everything is free—there are specific titles that are offered, but these
are wonderful to help build our classroom libraries. My family has
a lot of fun each year as we dress as our favorite heroes, get to meet
authors and artists, and participate in other fun activities with our
local shop.

Single Panel—Often, all we need is to share a single panel from a comic.
Use one panel or cover from a comic and put it on the smartboard
and use it to spark a conversation—I have used this one from
Batman, having the image on the smartboard, and simply ask the
students to discuss in small groups and let the conversation go from
there. How does this comic reflect our society and/or current events?
(Image 3.1 Batman Profiling).

Gather what you can—Have different comics on the same type of topic.
For instance, students could be separated into small groups to read
and booktalk a comic on persecution, another group reads a different
subject, etc. This way, you could make the most out of your budget
by having a few copies of multiple titles. This will also allow for
student choice as they can read the book that they most want to read.
The groups can then report on what they read, share a favorite few
panels, and have a class conversation on their findings.

Donations—don't underestimate the power of asking for donations.
Talk to your local comic book store owner and ask for donations
and even for old promotion posters that they are no longer using.
Publishers, and creators, LOVE to hear that their work is being used
in classrooms. Approach them on social media, at conferences, etc.—
but also offer how you plan to use their materials in the classroom.
Publicize their work on social media and in reviews—make this a
mutually beneficial relationship. I can't overstate the importance
of having a business card, yes, as an educator. Take full advantage

Image 3.1 **Batman Racial Profiling**
Batman #44 DC Comics 2015. Art by Jock (Mark Simpson), Scott Snyder author

of conversations when at a conference and leave your contact information behind.

Digital Comics—there are fantastic resources online to find digital comics, both past and present. Sure, when you find a comic from the 1960s that directly addresses racism, you can go to eBay and spend a lot of money to obtain a copy. Or you can use ComiXology, an online app that allows easy (and cheap) access to many titles of comics and graphic novels. DC and Marvel comics also offer online digital libraries of most of their titles.

In Chapter 5, I will showcase a lesson that uses inexpensive comics I have found at garage sales, flea markets, and in sales bins in stores.

4

How to Read Comics

One of the earliest learning moments I had when first integrating comics into my lessons was that some students were missing what I thought were obvious parts of the stories. Some of my most advanced readers were even saying that they didn't like comics because they didn't seem to make any sense. It took me a moment to realize why. Turns out, even in a classroom of 16–18-year-old students, many had never even held a comic before, let alone read one. As a Reading Specialist, I should have known better. I spend a lot of time in the beginning of the schoolyear showing my students HOW to read and analyze different types of text—poems, textbooks, etc.—and I firmly believe that all educators, no matter the level, need to do this more often. I realized that I needed to show students HOW to read a comic, just like I did with other mediums and types of literature. This reminds me of a story that I always tell about my oldest daughter and her experience during her first Reading Olympics competition (a PA, state-level reading competition club—your state likely has one, but with a different name). Pinch me—as a father, my kids LOVE to read everything and even join clubs where they read books to compete against other school districts in their understanding of these books! So proud! Following one competition, my daughter, Charlotte, came home to excitedly tell me about her experience. Turns out that many of her competitors were not able to answer some of the questions from that year's selection of graphic novels as they were based on the images. These advanced readers had not been taught HOW to read comics and so only looked at the text/dialogue, thereby missing much of the meaning of the story. One of the examples was

DOI: 10.4324/9781003291671-4

Wrinkle in Time, A: The Graphic Novel, adapted by Hope Larson, Farrar Straus Giroux, 2012. As a family, we read the original prose, the graphic novel, and watched the movie—we then did a text-to-text comparison between the different forms. My daughter was well prepared to answer these questions, and this gave me further insight into teaching with comics in my own classroom.

As this book is not a deep dive on the elements of comics themselves, but rather how to teach with comics, I will just go over the basics. I would encourage you to read Scott McCloud's *Understanding Comics* (William Morrow 1993) if you want to delve deeper into the literary elements of comics. In my classroom, the starting point is to show a few comics' pages on the smartboard before we begin reading comics. Just the basics, but I also get into the importance of how the images add depth and meaning to the story. We will point to specific information in the panels, such as body language, facial expression, background, even shading. Too many times, students will just skip past the pages without text, not realizing that these pages often have the most depth. I also do this when we begin a new comics lesson in the classroom—I will show one image and take it apart. When the students work on their lessons, I also have them do the same. As previously discussed, the skills transfer is wonderful in picking apart political cartoons, giving textual evidence in prose, understanding infographics, identifying techniques used in advertising, everything we want our 21st-century learners to do when analyzing text.

The most basic terms to understand when reading comics:

Comic books and graphic novels are understood to basically be the same thing. Some like to use the term graphic novel because it seems to add more literary weight to the medium. However, this term can be confusing—what about non-fiction graphic novels, graphic memoirs, etc.? In my opinion, the major difference is that comic books are shorter and tend to tell an incomplete story as they are serialized. Graphic novels (of any genre) are longer-form comics and tend to tell a complete story.

Z-Pattern—in general, comics are read in the same manner as prose— left to right and up to down, forming a Z-pattern. This basic structure will help the reader navigate more complicated pages, such as a splash page. In manga, the reading format is right to left but still up to down.

Panel—this is the basic structure of each part of the story. A panel is often square, but can be any shape, and sometimes does not have any specific structure or defined borders. This is one particular snapshot in time.

Splash Page—this can be either one page or a two-page spread. Often, this is an action-packed part of the story, and there can be a lot going on in this space. The reader needs to slow down and look at what is going on here. There may be inset panels and dialogue going on around the central image.

Gutter—this is the space between panels. Sounds simple, but it is important to understand that much often happens in this blank space. This is a great way to teach about story structure and how stories "move"—what happened in this blank space? How did the character get from one situation to another? We have had some great conversations in my classroom as students share their opinions.

Dialogue Balloon—the tail of the balloon will point to the character who is doing the speaking—either out loud or to themselves. These balloons can take many forms and add depth to the story in powerful ways. A jagged-edged balloon can denote anger or fear. A cloud shape can show that the character is having an inner monologue. Within these balloons, don't overlook the power of lettering—the formatting of the actual words. Just like in prose, words can be underlined, bolded, even slanted to get across meaning to the reader.

Caption—this is a block of text that can be from the narrator, an inner monologue, etc.

Some other things to pay attention to while reading—how color/shading can be used to denote emotion, facial expression, body language, items in the background, etc.

Once these basic terms are understood, readers will be able to understand the many different styles of comics. Just like when reading prose, successful readers will pause and go back when confused in a certain section of reading. Additionally, many comics publishers understand the importance of showing how to integrate their publications in the classroom and provide teacher resources online. I have written many educator guides for publishers, a collection of which can be found in the appendix to this book (titles such as: *Speak* by Laurie Halse Anderson / Emily Carroll, *American Born Chinese* by Gene Luen Yang, *A Wrinkle In Time* by Madeleine L'Engle/Hope Larson, *Real Friends/Best Friends* by Shannon Hale and LeUyen Pham, *Olympians* by George O'Connor, *Be Prepared* by Vera Brosgol). These guides are helpful in both learning how to read and how to teach comics.

Image 4.1 Speak

From SPEAK: THE GRAPHIC NOVEL by Laurie Halse Anderson; illustrations by Emily Carroll. Text copyright © 1999 by Laurie Halse Anderson. Pictures copyright © 2018 by Emily Carroll Reprinted by permission of Farrar Straus Giroux Books for Young Readers. All Rights Reserved.

Image 4.2 American Born Chinese
From AMERICAN BORN CHINESE by Gene Luen Yang. Copyright © 2006 by Gene Luen Yang. Reprinted by permission of First Second, an imprint of Roaring Brook Press, a division of Holtzbrinck Publishing Holdings Limited Partnership. All Rights Reserved.

Image 4.3 Wrinkle In Time
From A WRINKLE IN TIME: THE GRAPHIC NOVEL by Madeleine L'Engle; adapted & illustrated by Hope Larson. Text copyright © 1962 by Crosswicks, Ltd. Pictures copyright © 2012 by Hope Larson. Reprinted by permission of Farrar, Straus Giroux Books for Young Readers. All Rights Reserved.

Image 4.4 Olympians Book 1 Zeus
From OLYMPIANS: ZEUS: KING OF THE GODS by George O'Connor. Copyright © 2010 by George O'Con-nor. Reprinted by permission of First Second, an imprint of Roaring Brook Press, a division of Holtzbrinck Publishing Holdings Limited Partnership. All Rights Reserved.

Using the original comics page written by me and wonderfully illustrated by Ryan Dunlavey (https://www.ryandunlavey.com/) (Image 4.5), we can not only teach HOW to read comics but also WHY they are needed in classrooms. I had an idea in my head about a classroom setting where a student was trying to read a comic, one that was on-topic but just in a different medium. The teacher only sees that the student is not "paying attention" as he is directing, and so confiscates the child's comic, causing her to become embarrassed and even resentful. The student goes home to a room full of books and is left wondering why her teacher had such an issue with the reading material. However, we then see the teacher reading the comic Action Presidents (a REAL comic by Ryan Dunlavey and Fred Van Lente, published by HarperAlley—my own kids and I LOVE this entire series!) and finally understanding the educational application. The next day, he then uses images from the book to reach his students in a way that he was not able to do with his traditional teaching technique. This entire comic is based on real-life scenarios with people in my own life, including my son. Let's walk through the comic to see how it can be used in the classroom.

Panel #1: Narration block/caption—this gives us the setting. We can see on the projection screen that the topic matches that in the prose block—American Revolution. We can see that it is close to 3:00—a traditional end-of-the-school-day time. Every student, except for the one reading the comic, is either asleep or disengaged. The teacher, clearly stressed and trying to get his point across (we have all been there LOL), seems to be angry and unapproachable. Then we see the main character, reading a comic as she hides behind another book, but she is excited and highly engaged with the material. We could ask students to describe the feelings of the characters and if they have ever had a similar experience in school. Students can discuss what they think will happen next and what they think SHOULD happen next if they were the teacher or student. In just one panel, we have a place and time (setting), main characters have been described, and we already have a sense of each character's personality. We feel emotionally involved in a setting in which most of us are familiar.

Panels 2 and 3: the student has been caught reading the comic. Students can then discuss their previous answers to panel #1 and see if the story follows their prediction. What happened in the gutter between panels 1, 2, and 3? How is the student feeling? Just as important—how are the OTHER students feeling? Give visual/textual evidence to describe their feelings (e.g., wide-eyes, frowns, worried eyebrows, body posture—rigid and straight, etc.). We can also ask students to draw the teacher—what does he look like outside of the panel? Students can also write a prose paragraph or a dialogue

Image 4.5 Dunlavey original image
Ryan Dunlavey https://www.ryandunlavey.com

balloon describing what the comic reader or the other students are thinking. What would have happened if the bell did not ring in panel 3?

Panel 4: How must the reader be feeling? Describe the look on her face and body posture. Once again, describe the teacher and what type of person he is. Predict—what is going to happen next?

Panel 5: Describe the room of the reader—what do you notice about it? What type of student and/or person do you think she is (well-organized, neat, many nooks, a desk with a computer, etc.)? How is she feeling? What do you think she should do? What would you do? Predict—what happens the next day in school? What happened in the gutter between panels 4 and 5? Did she talk to her parents or friends about it? How about between panels 5 and 6? Did she sleep at all? Blog about it on her computer?

Panel 6: describe the teacher—how is he feeling? Why? What is the significance of the images in the dialogue balloon and the lines drawn around him? Look at the circle inset between this panel and panel #3—why did the artist of this comic choose to zoom in on the cover of the book? How is it connected? Now predict what you think will happen the next day in school. What happens in the gutter between panels 6 and 7?

Panel 7: Compare this to the first panel—what are the differences? Why? Why is the word shared put into quotation marks? Pay attention to the small details—is the fact that the teacher is no longer wearing a tie a reflection of his new approach to teaching? Is his shirt untucked? Importance? Describe his body posture as compared to panel #1. In what ways was this experience beneficial for the teacher and students? Could we have misjudged the teacher? Was he always this unapproachable, or do you think he was either just having a bad day or just unaware of the power of comics?

Wrap-up: Write a paragraph or two describing your reaction to the comic and any connection you were able to make in your own life. Do you think this is a realistic ending? How might you have changed the ending? (You can have students draw their own final panel.) Have the students draw an entire comic about an experience in their school day that they would change if given the opportunity and voice. (I LOVE when students feel comfortable giving me new ideas on how to teach/run the classroom—it is so powerful when they feel seen and heard. Plus, I get to learn as well!)

Whew! All of this from just one page! I have read this comic many times and have gotten new information each time I have looked at it! That's the beauty of comics—so much is up to the eye of the beholder, and wonderful conversations erupt about what students are seeing. Be open to new interpretations as students find their confidence in their own personal opinions based on evidence. Sure, comics can often be read quickly, but once students understand the depth of the art and what is added to the story, they will become more of a close reader. These skills obviously translate into annotation of prose, poems, songs, political cartoons, advertisements, etc. Not only will students be able to understand how to read a comic with this activity, but the door to powerful conversations can also be opened in terms of how to help students become invested in what happens during the school day. Conversations like these will empower them and, hopefully, encourage our young people to become civically engaged.

5

Comics as Artifact

As mentioned before, cost is an important consideration when planning lesson resources, and comics are no different. On the first or second day of school, I implement an engaging, meaningful, and thoughtful lesson that costs about $30. Instead of giving out my syllabus, the textbook, and discussing why students must fear me—I want to open the door to making history more relatable with the idea that everything around us impacts the historical record. History is not just towering "great" men and women, diary entries, and items found in an archaeological dig. When the students leave my class during the first week of school, they are excitedly talking about the class, and I often get emails from enthusiastic parents and promises of visits during back-to-school night because the parents are interested in the lesson!

The lesson resources consist of comics from different decades with a focus on representation and change. These comics have been purchased from sale bins (often $1 each) at the comic store, flea markets, garage sales, and many have also been donated. I am purposeful in the comics I include as I want students to be able to compare similar characters throughout multiple decades. As an example, I include a comic of the traditional Thor and the Mighty Thor (Jane Foster), traditional Peter Parker Spider-Man and Miles Morales Spider-Man, etc. I don't always have a direct counterpart, but I want these comparisons to happen whenever possible. I also look for comics that will be

DOI: 10.4324/9781003291671-5

engaging—great covers, popular characters, etc. (I have done entire lessons analyzing comic book covers and analyzing them as societal artifacts, just like with the comics as described below.) There are also many comics that truly do represent the issues of the time, such as in (Image 5.1) Superman Vol 1 #408: *The Day the Earth Died*, March 14, 1985. (Cover artists Ed Hannigan and Al Williamson, DC Comics.) I remember how much the cover of this comic freaked me out as an 11-year-old kid!

Day 1—The students are given the following worksheet to answer the previous day, with these questions:

1. **What is a historical artifact? What are some examples?**
2. **How can historians use these artifacts to tell us about civilizations?**

Students pair/share their answers. After I showed them some military helmets, WWII currency with Hawaii printed on the back, WWII civilian English gas masks, etc., we discussed what these items can tell us about a society. The students took turns asking questions about the artifacts and making predictions. By high school, they had been well prepared in this process of analyzing historical artifacts, and their curiosity is always piqued with hands-on lessons.

Day 2—When students come in, there are two piles of comics on each table (my room is set up in a collaborative format with tables of four students). The students are asked not to touch the books on their desks, but they are already talking about them. I do spend a few minutes on respecting materials, especially NOT folding back the pages of the comics! Ugh! LOL. Some adults have expressed concern to me that I let students use my personal materials, but I have found it to work quite well. In fact, I believe that it helps create a classroom feeling of mutual respect, and it encourages students to bring in their own materials to share in class. The students are then asked to take out the Day 1 worksheet, compare their answers again, then choose a comic to read and reevaluate their Day 1 answers. They are instructed to read the comics as artifacts and to make a guess about the society that created this artifact. The two piles are purposefully constructed—one has "older" comics, and one has "newer" comics. The students are given some time to peruse the piles, but two students have to choose from one pile, and two from the other. This is important as the lesson is not as impactful if students all choose comics from the same general time period. They then answer the following questions before reading the comics:

Image 5.1 Superman Atomic War cover
Superman #408, The Day the Earth Died. March 14, 1985. DC Comics. Ed Hannigan and Al Williamson cover artists. Paul Kupperberg and Ed Hannigan authors.

Worksheet Part 2:

1. If you have a favorite superhero, comic series, or graphic novel, please list below. (I asked this so that I can make connections to titles already being read.)
2. Overall, what is your opinion of comic books? Why? (I was surprised that some students had never before read a comic book.)
3. As a class of historians, is it acceptable to use comic books as historical artifacts? In other words, can we learn about social studies through these sources? Explain why or why not—be sure to include specific examples (we can learn about _____ by reading comic books. We cannot learn about history through comic books because _____).

Worksheet Part 3—the students fill this out when reading the comic. This also gives me a chance to discuss the importance of proper citations when conducting research. I often have to go around to different students as it can sometimes be challenging to find this information as the "title page" is often not in the very front in comics.

1. Title of Comic:
2. Author and Illustrator:
3. Publishing Company:
4. Copyright Date
5. Let's assume that a reader can learn a lot about a society by reading its comic books. What can your comic tell you about the society in which it was published? Bullet SPECIFIC examples from the comic to showcase your findings.

Worksheet Part 4
Directions: when you have finished critically analyzing your comic book, pair/share your information with a partner. Answer the questions below.

1. Name of Partner:
2. What is your partner's opinion about comic books?
3. What information did he/she give you about the comic book that helped you analyze the society? Did your partner give you any new insight into how to analyze your comic book?
4. What do you and your partner think about using comic books as historical resources? Explain.

Worksheet Part 5—students share out answers to the large group, with most being that comics are not reliable artifacts and not much was able to be discerned about the civilization in which they were published. I then put some specific things to look for on the smartboard and have students go back and re-read the same comic, this time looking for examples of these topics. The answers begin to change, and students begin to understand that artifacts are all around us and not just letters from George Washington, etc. Some of my examples that I ask students to seek:

> Look at advertisements—technology, costs, etc.
> Read letters to the editor.
> Look for themes—violence?
> Historical tie-ins—what was going on in the country at that time it was published?
> How are women treated?
> What are the ethnicities of the main characters? Examples of representation?
> What's missing?
> Dye colors/quality of paper and drawing.
> How people are dressed/hairstyles.
> Digital Editions.
> Technology—Atari 2600 VS Playstation 4.

After this rereading, students begin to give some very detailed answers, including visual and textual evidence—again, these skills transfer across the curriculum. Some examples of past answers from students show the variety of thinking that these comics can inspire:

> "I used to think comic books were just for entertainment reads for kids. I was never interested in reading one and I have yet so far. I just never had the chance to read one . . . it is acceptable to use comics as artifacts. In Spider-Man, he used to swing from the Twin Towers, then when 9/11 happened, they created a comic of the towers exploding. Comic books can be based off of historical events and be very useful to learn about social studies."
> "Racial profiling—Super Sikh is seen as dangerous because of what he looks like. Modern day—racism towards Super Sikh because of his race and clothing."—*Super Sikh, April 2015*
> "Comic books can show a ton of historical information upon examination. The setting, protagonists, antagonists can show the mindset of the writers at the time and help us understand what the

past was like. Ex—Captain America punches Hitler—show that Nazis were the enemy at the time). . . . Many of the protagonists are women—this shows a very gender-equal mindset. Wolverine tells her allies that killing for revenge is wrong. This may reflect the invasion of Iraq after 9/11."

"In this comic, women are the powerful ones, they are the main characters and they are very strong. It shows that in this society, women have a strong role and there is gender equality. In the comic, they use a laptop, a cellphone, and high tech weapons. There are advertisements for ABC and Netflix, which shows a lot about entertainment in 2016. There is a link to a website and a digital copy of the comic. The comic also shows social media"—*Wolverine: the Startling Conclusion of the Four Sisters. Tom Taylor. May 2016.*

"The women at the start seem to be seducing Thor. It ends up being a trap. The men are the muscular and powerful ones while the women seem to take the role of pampering Thor—gender roles! When it cuts to a scene in the suburbs, the mother's children are playing ball. In modern day, they would see these kids most likely inside using technology . . . No black people in this comic. Summary—this comic/society glorifies strong white men."

"This comic focuses mostly on minorities which shows that the society either needed to empower them or are celebrating them. It features a black woman kicking butt (which is what black women do!), but this may tell that the society may have needed to see that a woman can be just as powerful as a man. It also shows a group of poor migrants in the desert trying to get into another land (USA?) to get jobs and settle, but some people stop them. They accuse them of being terrorists and job stealers and they say that they are going to build a wall. The people stopping them threaten to use violence . . . actually they are intent on using violence. This may show/depict real world events such as border control and illegal immigration. Then Captain America comes to try and let them through by beating up the other guys, which shows the author's opinion on the topic. Cap is arrested by others—this show racial profiling in society. Summary—This society needs to realize the good and power in both African Americans and women."—*Sam Wilson, Captain America.*

"Newer print, more colors, better paper. The main character is a woman, so it shows how women have gained power. References to current shows like Scooby Doo. Ivy is raising three kids on her own, which is now common for there to be single mothers. Stem cells. Hovering parents, who want the best for their children. "—*Poison Ivy, Amy Chu—August 2016.*

"Mentions issues in the 'corner' which is a rough neighborhood. Issues with cops shooting black males. Could allude to problems happening in this time period—police brutality, protests, etc. A hierarchy—the actions of the rich affect the society of the poor."—*Batman. Scott Snyder. 9/26/15.*

". . . with comic books from the fifties and sixties, you can see social and gender norms (the woman is the damsel in distress while the man is the super hero). . . . Godzilla was made partly because we were worried about the radioactive effects of Hiroshima and Nagasaki. . . . Can see the technology of the time—'operator? I need the number for X-Factor Headquarters in New York'. Shows how they couldn't just search up a number on the internet. You can tell a lot about gender roles/norms, because even though there is Marvel Girl, the male superheroes ultimately save the day. Marvel Girl gets a simple nosebleed and the male superheroes worry about her, but she wasn't seriously hurt. Also, the male superheroes are called MEN, but the woman is Marvel GIRL, which shows the damsel in distress role." Sum up the society in a sentence or two—"A society where men and women can band together, but are still not truly equal"—*The Incredible Hulk VS X-Factor, October 1987—Peter David and Todd Mcfarlane.*

Suddenly, students begin to see patterns and to question the representation in source material in all forms as we study history. One answer that really gave me pause was when a student wrote that she could tell the comic was from an older society as the kids were all outside playing and not inside on devices! Ugh. As an introductory lesson, this really allows the students and me to get to know one another in a fun and engaging way. Additionally, it sets up class norms and expectations of visual and textual evidence, group collaboration, and thinking deeply and on a personal level.

6

Some Quick and Easy Comics Lessons for Any Classroom

The previous chapter was an example of a specific lesson in my classroom, but this book is more about you adapting comics lessons as they best fit your classroom. Below are some generic lessons that can be as in-depth or introductory as you see fit. Again, this is not about replacing your traditional classroom resources but enhancing them.

> **Prediction/Summary**—have students stop at a point in the story and draw what they think happens next. It could be the next second, month, year, or even decade. (I will show a specific example in Chapter 10.) I would never grade students on artistic ability and am sure to explain this to them—stick figures are just fine! It's all about the storytelling. The same idea can be used to summarize a reading. When we read the *March* graphic novel, I have my students first analyze the cover of the book, and we discuss what we think we will be reading about. Asking questions is so important as an active reader and an activity for which I always make time. Why is it titled **March**? Why do we see so many walking? Where are they going? What types of people are walking? Who are the people sitting down? Why is the "counter closed"? Describe the looks on people's faces—what are they thinking? What is going to happen? (Image 6.1 March). I also often stop during climactic parts in the book as well to discuss and predict what will happen next. As an example, I stop my students on page 7, just as John Lewis and followers are

DOI: 10.4324/9781003291671-6

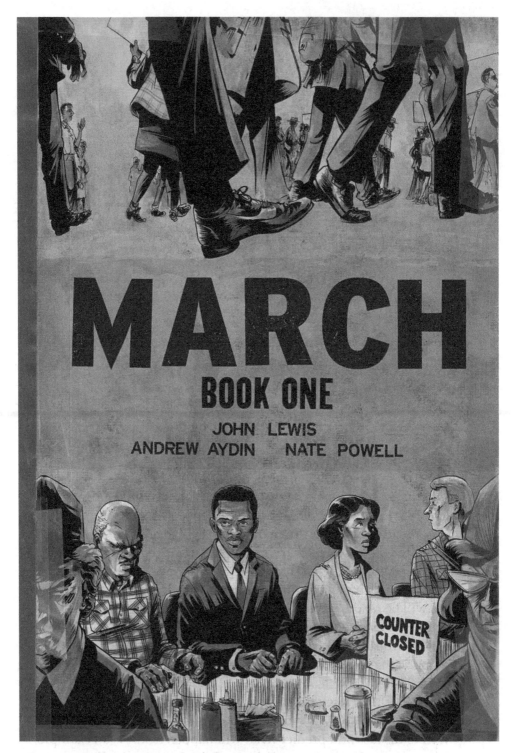

Image 6.1 March cover and page
March: Book One © John Lewis and Andrew Aydin, courtesy Top Shelf Productions/IDW Publishing.

Image 6.2 March cover and page
March: Book One © John Lewis and Andrew Aydin, courtesy Top Shelf Productions/IDW Publishing.

cresting the Edmund Pettus bridge and see the waiting police force on the other side. This is a powerful way to not only incorporate previous knowledge, but also to make an educated prediction. It also brings the students into the story in a very personal manner. Why do some of the word balloons have jagged edges? How are the people feeling? What are they thinking? We can't make out the words in some of the balloons; what do you think the people are saying? Why do the people in front kneel down? What would you do? What happens next? Students can write the answers to these questions or draw them. Many choose to draw the next panel (or several panels) using a simple sketch and even with stick figures (Image 6.2 March) (Image 6.3 March, Smyth—this was created by Liam Smyth, an eighth grade student).

Pre-writing—My students write a lot in my class—poems, essays, research papers, reflections, etc. In my discussions with college professors, I have found that one of the biggest challenges students have is the ability to create an organized and complete argument in a writing sample. It's not the content that is of the biggest concern, it is the writing. I teach all levels of students, including Advanced Placement, and find that much of these issues stem from not pre-writing. When students are assigned a five-page paper to write, they conduct some great research placed on note cards and then often just sit down to type the paper. However, the argument is often not clear, becomes repetitive, and important information is left out as the argument wanders without a strong thread. It can be challenging to have students pre-write as it seems like just another task, an additional burden. However, once this becomes an expectation in the classroom, once its importance is explained, it will become habit. One compelling way to introduce or reinforce this concept is by giving the students a specific amount of blank comic panels to use to summarize a reading or to plan out their own writing. It is easy to create the blank comic panels—create blocks in word, google "blank comic page", etc. There are also even selections of blank comic panels in collected books. The level of this challenge can be increased by adding in specific dialogue balloons in several panels. This forces students to pre-write and think deeply about what they want to say before beginning to write. (Again, these skills transfer!)

Filling in the blanks—what happens in the gutters? Have students either write or draw an explanation of what happens between two important panels in a comic. Create a comic panel to explain what happens between chapters in a prose book.

Image 6.3 **March—Liam Smyth**

Dialogue— Give students comics with the dialogue missing. Students are then tasked with filling in the dialogue between characters and then comparing it to the original comic. This can also be used with photographs or paintings of individuals and/or events. Have students place dialogue balloons, or thought bubbles, into a painting of Napoleon crossing the Alps. What's he thinking? Why? This is easy to do in PowerPoint (or other software) by uploading an image and blocking out the text, photocopying a comic with cardstock blocking the text, or just conducting an online search for "blank dialogue comics". This is a great lesson to use with langue learners!

Visual Evidence—this can be an extension to the previous dialogue task. When analyzing a comic, ask students to describe the thinking and/or emotions of a character. Pay attention to body language, facial expression, shape of the dialogue balloon, etc. These skills will transfer when analyzing political cartoons and other mediums when asked to produce specific evidence. Students will interpret visual and textual evidence in different ways, and that is exactly what we want. These discussions are often passionate as students defend their use of evidence and their interpretation. This is also a great lesson to use with language learners!

7

Sequencing and Personal Interpretation

Some of my worst experiences as a student happened when my teachers had students analyze text, such as a poem, and were then graded on our interpretation of the text. Often, students were marked incorrect because their interpretation disagreed with that of the teacher or even with the original author. There was no chance to explain the answer, just a red mark and points taken off. I want my students to understand that so much is up to the reader and that their interpretation, backed up with evidence, is valid. A poem, or a song, is a living, breathing creature and changes in the minds of each individual and what background they bring with them. Stories are interpreted differently by different generations, by readers from different backgrounds, etc. As a social studies teacher, this is so important to understand. History is not just a collection of facts—there is much interpretation, and meanings change as these "facts" are discussed and further researched. We read and annotate poetry and music as artifacts in my social studies classroom to better understand the time period or event. As an example, we analyze Wilfred Owens when learning about the humanity of WWI. Students often disagree with my interpretation and one another on the meaning of individual lines, or even of entire overall meanings of the artifact—and that's ok. Students just have to show me why they think this way. Convince me. Provide evidence from the text. Another great example is *"Every Breath You Take"*—a total stalker song that some misinterpret and use as a wedding song! Sting has discussed this in many interviews explaining that he doesn't understand this choice, but he does know that songs, once written and produced, take on a life of their own and mean different things to different people.

DOI: 10.4324/9781003291671-7

With this skill in mind, I have found the following lesson idea to be a highly successful way to teach about personal interpretation and story sequencing. This activity also showcases the power of the gutter between each panel as the reader has to understand what happens in the space between panels to properly organize them and to make a coherent story. Whenever I work with elementary students, I LOVE to see their eyes light up when they understand that their interpretation truly matters. I have several popular comic pages printed and laminated, ones that my students have created or favorite pages from books I own. When choosing a comic, it is best to choose one that has no words, or as few as possible. I then cut up each individual panel and attach a Velcro fastener to the back of each. I also have a brightly colored board to which we will attach each panel. You can use a small whiteboard, a picture frame, etc. On the back of the board, I attach a second copy of the same comic in its original entirety. When the student begins the task, they will have a small pile of laminated comic panels, and their task is to analyze them and attach them to the board in the order they think best tells the story of the comic.

Once their version of the story is completed, I then turn the board around to show the original comic. Often, the new version differs from the original, and the participant can look disappointed as though they failed the task. However, I encourage them to share with me their story—to explain the order they chose. Their interpretation is valuable, adds to the story, and can be better than the original. Once they understand that their story idea is valued, they are then encouraged to try to make up as many different versions as possible. They can continue to unhook and rehook the laminated panels and then explain how the story has changed. It is fun to just change the first and last panels to see how they can change the entire meaning of the story. Students can then be tasked with writing the accompanying story to their version of the comic or to fill in the dialogue.

We can use this image from Mark Grenier (Image 7.1) to understand how this sequencing lesson can work. Once these images are cut out, we can make many different stories, each with a different meaning. One version might begin with the angry adult (Dad? Pop Pop?) giving the kid a hard time about playing in the leaves when there is work to be done. The kid maybe then runs for a rake and excitedly runs back to help the adult. Or maybe the story begins with the middle panel of leaves falling into a pile and then the kid kids jumping in. There really are so many possibilities, and students can also draw a similar story about their lives, cut it out, and have students guess their original order.

Image 7.1 **Mark Grenier**

Ways to Modify This Lesson

> Literary/story elements—which panel contains rising action—unhook it and write a three-sentence description of what is happening. Which panel is the most important? Why?
>
> Science experiments—what is the correct order of the experiment? What might happen if the order is changed?
>
> Film—storyboarding and story arc
>
> Social Studies—change the order of an event—what would change?

You can also go back to Chapter 4 and use the American Revolution classroom comic for this activity. Switch up the panels and see how it changes the story. If we take panel #7 (the happy ending) and put it before panel #1 (the angry teacher), the meaning becomes quite different. It begins with an open-minded teacher and engaged students, who then completely change. What might have happened between the panels? Did a principal or parent complain about the use of comics?

Another comic I use to teach about personal interpretation and sequencing incorporates multiple illustrators' interpretations of several Bob Dylan songs. In *Bob Dylan Revisited: 13 Graphic Interpretations of Bob Dylan's Songs*, W. W. Norton & Company, 2009, students can visually see how illustrators interpreted Dylan's songs in various ways. When we study the songs of the 60s and protest music, students listen to many songs of the time period and explain their interpretation of the lyrics. To really help them envision their own interpretations, we first listen to the songs depicted in *Bob Dylan Revisited*) and annotate the prose lyrics. Students then read and annotate the visual interpretations in the book and discuss how they differed from their own. I find it best to use sticky notes to annotate the comic panels so students can directly point to specific evidence. Later, students will choose a song that they connect with from the time period and create their own comic interpretation.

8

Symbolism and Culture

Naming a character Captain America has a certain weight and cultural importance, especially when he famously debuted by punching Hitler in the face. But what does Captain American really represent? What is symbolic about his uniform or how he's presented? Does he have to be a white male? After fielding observations, turn this over to students and have them create their own version of Captain America. Have them explain their depictions. Of course, for those who read the comics, we already know that there have been many people who have taken up the shield, such as Sam Wilson and Isaiah Bradley, Samantha Wilson, Roberta Mendez, Danielle Cage, and the newest (June 2021), Aaron Fischer, who also happens to be gay. Similarly, I open the school year with asking students to mentally imagine the average American and to draw that person (including home, clothing, accessories, etc.). This leads us into a conversation about the actual make-up of America and why many students draw a straight, two-parent white family in a suburban home. We look at the US census and other data to highlight the wondrous diversity in the United States. Students then create their own individual Captain America. (I choose NOT to discuss the different Captain Americas in the comics as I do not want to interfere with their creative process, but I do show them afterwards.) I give some ideas to be included in the drawing and explain their choices. Uniform and colors, accessories, superpowers, origin story, even teammates and enemies. This engaging lesson incorporates the ideas of symbolism, culture, nationalism, and story-telling. We then discuss what Captain America would look like in 50 years, 100 years, 200 years ago, etc.

DOI: 10.4324/9781003291671-8

I also adapt this lesson for my Global History course in making a Captain _____ for different areas of the world. What would Captain Mexico look like? Captain Sri Lanka? This is a great way to introduce culture and regions to students of all ages. After conducting research, students create their hero to best represent the culture they are assigned or have been allowed to choose. The origin story of the hero comes from students researching the early history of this area. Students often include national animals as hero pets and have a lot of fun with it.

There are many ways to adapt this lesson for all classes. Imagine Major Mitosis, Colonel Calculus, General Geography, or even Super Stretch in Physical Education. Create a hero or illustration for each element on the Periodic Table. You can even take a literary character and turn them into a hero. There are already wonderful examples of this being done to inspire this process. I love the teen math hero team of solutionsquad.net—created by middle school math teacher Jim McClain (Images 8.1–8.3). We have had a lot of fun making these heroes—even having class and district-wide voting on the most impressive. These heroes can then be 3-D printed to make actual action figures! This is a perfect cross-curricular STREAM project.

I am also a consultant with the US State Department and have been lucky enough to be a part of an inspiring educational experience. I have had the pleasure of working alongside Jacquie Gardy (@jacquiegardy), Jennifer Williams (@JenWilliamsEdu), and Dan Ryder (@WickedDecent) as we put together a virtual exchange program for educators around the world! We help facilitate a conversation about American culture through comics, how to read and use comics in the classroom, and how to show students how to make original comics. We have the educators and their students create their own national superhero as described above. The participants then have their hero solve both local and national issues. However, we add to this lesson by having participants from different areas of the world interact with one another and have their heroes help solve issues in the other's country. The pairs/groups then work together and create an original comic. (I will discuss more about how to create comics later in Chapter 16.) This cultural exchange is fun and powerful as we discover how much we actually have in common as a global community. Many of the local issues brought up in these discussions are actually shared global issues of equality, environmental issues, access to education, etc. When creating these comics, we find that this visual literacy really breaks down any language or cultural barriers and that comics truly are universal.

Another adaptation of this lesson is to have students create a hero out of a historical or cultural figure. Too often, we just don't have the time to discuss enough important people that impact us. In this lesson, students can

Image 8.1 **Jim McClain**
Jim McClain, founder of SolutionSquad.net

Image 8.2 Jim McClain
Jim McClain, founder of SolutionSquad.net

Image 8.3 Jim McClain
Jim McClain, founder of SolutionSquad.net

either choose a person they feel needs more attention in education, they can be given a list from which to choose, or they can be assigned a person. This lesson can be as broad or as narrow as you would like—it could be for AAPI Heritage Month, for those who have advanced science, etc. I enjoy giving students a self-created list of civil rights leaders throughout American History once we have finished reading the March Trilogy. These leaders have fought for the rights of Hispanic, LGBTQIA+, female, handicapped, Asian, and many more Americans throughout time, including today. Suddenly, we have over 30 biographies created and discussed in the classroom and have opened many powerful discussions.

This lesson can also be extended to other characters, such as Spider-Man, Super Man, and Green Lantern. Peter Parker has been joined by Spider-Gwen, Miles Morales, Miguel O'Hara, Pavitr Prabhakar (from India), and even Peter Porker as Spider-Ham! A quick online search will provide approximately 100 different types of "Spider-Men"! My favorite is Spider-Man Noir, who was alive during the Great Depression. The same can be found for other popular heroes—Super-Man is not always white, such as with Calvin Ellis, who is Black, or Kong Kenan, who is Chinese. Wonder Woman has a Black twin sister, Nubia. The Green Lantern Corps has much representation, including Simon Baz, who is a Lebanese-Arab American and Muslim, and Jessica Cruz, who is both Mexican-American and Honduran-American. These are just some of the characters students can research and use as inspiration to create their own hero. Who is missing? Who is not being represented? The idea of representation in comics can be a research project unto itself! As Miles Morales said at the end of Spider-Man: Into the Spider-Verse (2018), "I never thought I'd be able to do any of this stuff. But I can. Anyone can wear the mask. You can wear the mask. If you didn't know that before, I hope you do now. Cuz I'm Spider-Man. And I'm not the only one. Not by a long shot."

Through my experiences with the US State Department comics program, I became even more aware of comics in other cultures. American heroes are well-known around the world, especially as a result of recent movies. This has always given my students and me wonderful and immediate connections when working with students from around the world. There is always an initial moment of hesitation when getting to know students on another continent through a computer screen. However, once the topic of comics and music come up, it is quick to realize that teenagers around the world really have so much in common. Once this initial introduction is completed, then we can delve more deeply into the pop culture of cultures from around the world. We have learned about Priya's Mask, India's first female superhero

Image 8.4 **Priya's Mask**
https://www.priyashakti.com/priyas-mask courtesy of Rattapallax

(https://www.priyashakti.com/priyas-mask), and the African heroes by the Nigerian comics company https://www.thecomicrepublic.com/ (Images 8.4 and 8.5).

I have also used this lesson idea for National Superhero Day, which occurs on April 28th. I ask students to think of someone in their life who they believe is a hero. I have had quite a few phone calls from my high school students' parents telling me through tears how impacted they were to be made into a superhero. We can also use this for Teacher Appreciation Week or other topics—there are almost limitless possibilities.

Image 8.5 Comic Republic

Art by Ireti Moremi courtesy of the Comic Republic https://www.thecomicrepublic.com/

9

Tough Topics

My daughter was in elementary school when she came home visibly upset and told me about a video she watched in class about 9/11. This video showed horrific images of people jumping from the burning towers, and she just couldn't process why this would happen. I tried to explain so much about that day, how we felt, the questions we had, and how we were able to go back to school the next day. She felt better, but I still didn't think that she was able to get past the mental images in her mind to understand what I was saying. I went into my comics bin and pulled out the *Amazing Spider-Man Volume 2 #36*, December 2001. Marvel comics take place in the real world, often in New York City. Following this tragedy, it was decided not to ignore the events of that day but rather to write them into the comics. This powerful comic opens up with Spider-Man at ground zero as the buildings collapse. Throughout the comic, there are moments of doubt and disbelief, civilians even questioning Spider-Man about how he could let this happen. This really encapsulates many of my feelings from that day—the most powerful nation in the world brought to its knees shook my idea of safety and security. But the comic continues to show the first responders and many others arriving to help. This is an honest look at the events of the day and shows how others reacted around the world. This comic, written by J. Michael Straczynski, penciled by John Romita, Jr., inked by Scott Hanna, and colored by Dan Kemp, enabled my daughter to make sense of an event that was beyond her young mind in an honest yet accessible way, and I am forever grateful as a father and educator. I now use this comic in my classroom every year to discuss not only

DOI: 10.4324/9781003291671-9

the events and history of that day, but also on comics as artifacts. This comic can be purchased online, but it can be pricey. However, digital copies can be purchased for $1.99 on Kindle at the time of this writing. (The entire lesson I use is included in the appendix of this book.)

In my high school classroom, this comic opens up discussions about 9/11 in a way that other mediums have not allowed to happen. This event has personal significance to me, but it is a distant event to many of my students. They have watched the videos, seen the newsclips, and read accounts of the day. To be honest, many have expressed a certain feeling of repetition as each September brings many of the same lessons. However, I have found that this Spider-Man comic, as a societal artifact, grabs the attention of students and jars them into asking important questions, not the least of which is why. This comic has us using Google Earth and GPS coordinates, discussing how this event impacted peoples around the world, and connecting to other artifacts from other impact-ful events. These activities go beyond marking a day and push my students to analyze and research. There are also many other examples about 9/11 in comics, not just from Marvel if you wanted to compare different depictions (Image 9.1—9–11: The World's Finest Comic Book Writers and Artists Tell Stories to Remember, DC Comics 2002, cover image by Alex Ross).

Another difficult topic that is always on the minds of those in education is school shootings. In the comic, *Champions #24*, September 2016 by Marvel Comics, a shooting occurs in Miles Morales's high school. The team—writer Jim Zub, artist Sean Izaakse, colorists Marcio Menyz and Erick Arciniega, and letterer Clayton Cowles, created a comic that made me, as an educa-tor, feel seen. After reading it, I immediately went back to the comics store and bought 30 copies of the book to share in our classroom. The impact was immediate—the fact that school shootings were now being written about in our comics spoke volumes about our society and current issues. This allowed us to have open, honest conversations in a way that reading a news story just could not. I met Jim Zub at a conference and just thanked him for truly show-ing the impact of these events on our schools. The lead into the book states, "The Champions grapple with a foe that all the superpowers in the world cannot vanquish!" Talk about an understatement. In the story, following the shooting, the school holds an active shooter drill. It causes so much trauma as one student cries through the drill and is held by a classmate. The story also has the teen heroes discussing what they can do about it and how they just feel so powerless. As the heroes discuss their options, students are also then encouraged to debate what can be done to keep these events from happening again and can inspire civic engagement.

Teaching about the Jewish Holocaust is another emotionally charged experience, but it is vital for understanding not only that genocide, but as a

Image 9.1 DC 9/11 Cover
9–11: The World's Finest Comic Book Writers and Artists Tell Stories to Remember, DC Comics 2002, cover image by Alex Ross

foundation for understanding other horrific events in history along with current events. In my students' Language Arts classes, amongst other literature, the students read *Night* by Elie Wiesel, and many have already read the *Diary of Anne Frank*. As a social studies teacher, I offer to support that understanding by providing historical context, but also by integrating the same literacy skills in my class. As a parent, I also understand the emotional impact that these tough topics have on our young people and know the need to thoughtfully approach the material and not just "cover" the history. Just as Spider-Man helped my daughter better understand 9/11, comics can also do the same for the Jewish Holocaust. In *Magneto: Testament*, by Greg Pak and Carmine Di Giandomenico, Marvel Comics, August 2014, we see the origins of Magneto and the development of his powers in a concentration camp. This powerful comic places a well-known villain in a historical context and forces the reader to consider why he makes the choices he does as an adult. This book comes with extensive resources for educators in an expanded appendix. In cinema, we see this origin in the movie *X-Men: First Class (2011)*, as Magneto's powers first appear when he is separated from his family at Auschwitz. I show this clip in class, and I am always amazed at the emotional power of this scene. As an adult, Magneto hunts down and kills these concentration camp guards. We hear him say, "I've been at the mercy of men just following orders. Never again." This will eventually lead us into reading excerpts from *Ordinary Men: Reserve Police Battalion 101 and the Final Solution in Poland* by Christopher R. Browning, Harper Perennial 2017. This is the enduring understanding that we want our students to leave with, not just the events, but how/why would people willingly carry out such orders?

Of course, there are now many powerful comics centering on the Jewish Holocaust, and I have many of them in my classroom. I don't have class sets, but perhaps one or two copies of each title, and students are welcome to read them during downtime, during study hall, or to borrow and take home. There are two different graphic adaptations of the *Diary of Anne Frank* that we discuss as we do a text-to-text-to-text comparison of the original prose diary and these two adaptations. (*Anne Frank's Diary: the Graphic Adaptation* by Ari Folman and David Polinsky, Pantheon Books 2018. *Anne Frank: the Anne Frank Authorized Graphic Biography* by Sid Jacobson and Ernie Colon, Hill and Wang 2010.) I also include children's books/picture books, as I do with most units. The idea is to give a wide sampling of different types of texts, including the traditional textbook, primary sources, and more. These visual connections stay with students and allow them to make meaningful connections across time periods as we later research modern genocides and their similarities. Of course, there is also the much respected *Maus* by Art Spiegelman—a graphic interpretation of the author's interviews with his father and his experiences in the Jewish Holocaust. I would also highly suggest purchasing *Meta Maus*, also by Art Spiegelman, Pantheon Books, 2011, as it is a treasure trove of historical documents and process that are an inseparable part of teaching Maus.

As teachers, we need to be able to tactfully discuss a variety of difficult topics. Rather than shy away from these conversations, I have found comic books to be an invaluable tool for opening up discussion while allowing students to delve deeper without being overly graphic or more traumatic than necessary.

10

Wordless Comics

Going back to the power of comics and visual literacy in encouraging individual interpretation, wordless comics are a powerful way to open the door to these skills. One of the most challenging skills to teach students is that their opinion truly does matter and that they don't have to agree with me or some unknown textbook editor. I encourage them to tell me their interpretation and that it is also okay to be wrong when shown evidence to the contrary. Lord knows I am wrong all the time. I am willing to change my mind when faced with specific textual or visual evidence. I use wordless comics in my classroom to underscore the importance of interpretation/opinion when using this specific evidence. My first experience with the application of this in education was with my daughter as we read together the wordless picture book about the Underground Railroad *Unspoken: A Story From the Underground Railroad* by Henry Cole, Scholastic Press 2012. This story focuses on a young white girl discovering a runaway slave hiding on her farm. Throughout, we see her struggling with whether or not she should become involved and help this young man.

In one particularly powerful image, we see a cornfield with just an eye peeking out from behind ears of corn. There are no distinguishing features, and the color is a washed yellow—so no way to definitely determine the ethnicity or gender of the character behind the corn. My daughter, Charlotte, who was in third grade at the time, and I disagreed on the identification of the character. As this is a wordless story, there was not even a narrator to help us with this identification. My daughter and I flipped pages back and forth

DOI: 10.4324/9781003291671-10

in an attempt to make a determination as we both pointed to specific visual evidence to back up our differing opinions. This is the power of comics and visual literacy—the reader needs to be much more introspective and self-reliant as there is no text to tell the reader what to think. My daughter and I had reached an impasse, and neither of us would back down. My daughter decided to look up the contact information for the author and emailed Mr. Cole. She explained the situation to the author and "demanded" to know who the character was behind the corn. To my immense pleasure, Cole not only emailed her back, but also responded that it was up to her to make a personal determination! This frustrated my daughter enough that she decided to write out the entire story in prose to prove her point, translating visual into textual evidence. She created a wonderful and compelling story, but more than that, learned a valuable lesson about being observant. Elementary teachers often use similar type lessons with picture books, but sadly some people tend to look down on these lessons in upper grades. Whether third grade or eleventh, asking students to investigate, analyze, and prove should be routine and can easily be practiced with wordless comics.

There are other wonderful examples of wordless comics, such as *The Arrival* by Shaun Tan, but I will focus on one here that I use extensively in my classroom. The skills can be transferred to any other wordless comic. In my Global History class, I use the stunning *Nat Turner* graphic novel by Kyle Baker, Abrams ComicArts, 2008, to teach about the impact of slavery and imperialism. This book is based on the text, *The Confessions of Nat Turner*, and the comic panels themselves are wordless. It is by focusing on the images and not words that students become emotionally involved in the events and make immediate and powerful connections to other events in history. I begin the lesson in a fairly "easy" way with the students—they are given a simple worksheet that has page numbers on it. Their task is to read the images and write a two-sentence summary for every two pages in the first chapter. I really don't have specific expectations for what they write—it could be questions, something that stuck out to them, an explanation of events, etc. I just want them interacting with the images and referring to specific visual evidence. This worksheet idea can be used with any comic lesson or really when interacting with any medium as it encourages individual interpretation. As this is a wordless comic, students will often come up to me or call me over, point to an image, and ask me what is happening. My response is always the same—"It's whatever you think it is." And I mean it—there really is not a wrong answer, as long as the student can point to specific evidence to defend their interpretation. Although my room is set up in collaborative tables of four students, and I always encourage discussions, I ask students to be quiet during this lesson. I don't want them to influence one another's answers. I want to build the self-confidence of students as individual thinkers. Too often, students have a school experience of memorizing the "right" answers and spitting them back out. I want my students to struggle a bit in this experience and not feel confident in their answers at first. I want them to know that having questions is a good thing, that not knowing is perfectly fine when learning. After they get through the first few pages, I model my interpretation on the smartboard. I have circled parts of the images to show the type of evidence I am seeking. I also have questions and ask students to help me interpret some of the images. As there are many answers, students begin to relax as they realize that I really am not looking for one thing in particular, and then they complete the task.

After everyone has finished reading and annotating (an admittedly sneaky way to teach this skill), we then have time for small group/pair share discussions before we share out to the larger group. This can also help alleviate anxiety and allow each student to have a voice, even if they do not feel comfortable sharing in a larger group setting. However, before they begin the discussions, they are told to put away their pens because I find that some students will change their answers to parrot those from others in the group. I want THEIR answers and to see THEIR thinking. As the students conduct their small group discussions, I walk around and sit at each table, listening, and occasionally commenting. I want to be able to interact with everyone on a more personal level instead of just standing in the front of the room. Often, I am impressed by their interpretations of the images. I am sure to share this reaction with the students and to tell them when they change my perception of a panel.

As students read, I also ask them to note any connections that they make because seeing connections is a mark of an active reader. Almost immediately, my students begin to make connections to the Jewish Holocaust as they see one rebellious woman literally have her humanity stripped away as her clothes are taken from her (Images 10.1–10.4). When she is then branded, students visualize the arm tattoos assigning human beings a number in the Nazi camps. We then later make connections reading about the Japanese-American internment camps during WWII and the number tags that were assigned to all who America interned. When seeing an illustration of the bowels of the cargo hold, students tell me that it reminds them of the picture of Elie Wiesel in the camps that they saw when reading *Night*. This is truly the power of visual literacy and comics and the immediate and deep connections made between texts. In just a few pages, students have gotten involved in historical events on a deeply personal level and feel responsible for the people they are seeing in the comics.

Image 10.1 **NAT TURNER**

From NAT TURNER by Kyle Baker. Copyright © 2008 Kyle Baker. Used by permission of Harry N. Abrams, Inc., New York. All rights reserved.

Image 10.2 NAT TURNER
From NAT TURNER by Kyle Baker. Copyright © 2008 Kyle Baker. Used by permission of Harry N. Abrams, Inc., New York. All rights reserved.

Image 10.3 NAT TURNER
From NAT TURNER by Kyle Baker. Copyright © 2008 Kyle Baker. Used by permission of Harry N. Abrams, Inc., New York. All rights reserved.

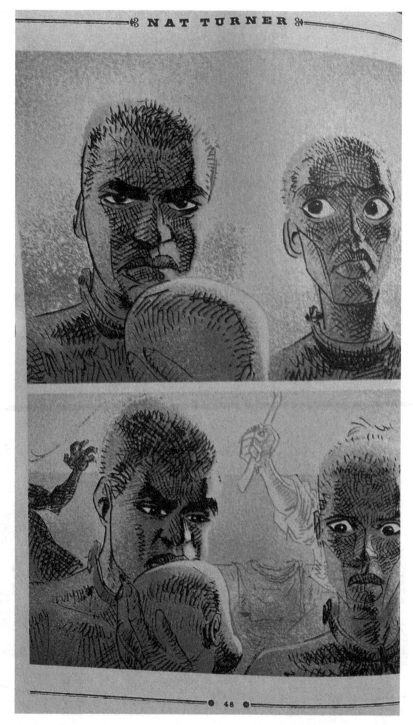

Image 10.4 **NAT TURNER**

From NAT TURNER by Kyle Baker. Copyright © 2008 Kyle Baker. Used by permission of Harry N. Abrams, Inc., New York. All rights reserved.

After reading and discussing the first 56 pages of Nat Turner, students are then tasked with drawing what they think will happen next. They can create one image or draw an entire comic. It can take place one minute after the last page or as far into the future as they imagine. Artistic skill doesn't matter here (although some students are able to really shine with the inspiring talent), as it is about the message/story-telling. Some students draw an auction where those who survived the Middle Passage are sold as property. Others will draw enslaved people working in the fields. Still others will draw a modern classroom, where the teacher is sharing the lives of these people to help end racism. As often as possible, we need to give students as much leeway as we can, and they will continue to surprise and inspire us (Image 10.5 Charlotte Smyth).

As a final part of this lesson, we also listen to some Hip Hop from the 90s and today to discuss the impact of race and slavery on the contemporary United States. How much has changed? What can this song (artifact) tell us about the time period when it was published? One song in particular, *Can't Truss It* by Public Enemy, leads to some powerful conversations and connections between these time periods and current racial issues. I also ask students to share songs they listen to today that make similar connections. There is also a powerful song by Reef the Lost Cauze titled "Nat Turner" that we listen to and annotate. Reef is a Philadelphia artist, and this also helps us to build connections as he lives in our area. The idea that Nat Turner educated himself to resist and rebel is a powerful message. The skills we learned in this lesson transfer throughout the rest of the year—making connections, asking questions, and creating interpretation with specific visual/textual evidence.

When we later begin learning about the Jewish Holocaust, we analyze some photos—nothing overwhelming and horrific as this will simply shut down many students. However, I do show some images that were taken in the Warsaw Ghetto during 1941, along with some others. The lesson begins with students being asked to create a list of questions about the photograph connected to specific visual evidence. The discussions in class are meaningful as the students are not afraid to ask questions and are ok with not knowing because of our earlier work with *Nat Turner* and personal interpretation. When we share the questions, students will point to specific parts of the photograph to try to help answer the questions. They take their time analyzing the photos as they did with the comic. They remember their earlier mental connections between this comic and the Jewish Holocaust. These skills are highly transferrable to also analyzing all sorts of mediums, including political cartoons, propaganda posters, etc. A few months after the Nat Turner lesson, I use another wordless comic to introduce WWI and the reality of trench warfare.

The Great War: July 1, 1916: The First Day of the Battle of the Somme by Joe Sacco (W. W. Norton & Company, November 4, 2013) is a comic unlike any other

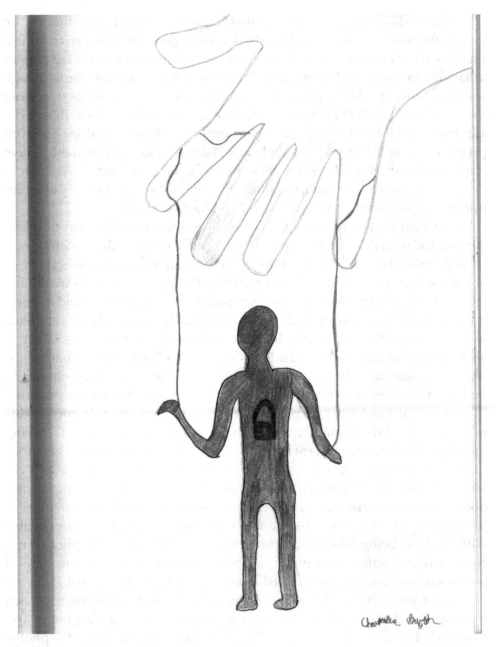

Image 10.5 Charlotte Smyth

I have ever read. It is a 24-foot-long comic that is more like a tapestry (I compare it to the Bayeux Tapestry—another comic) that details the first 24 hours of the Battle of the Somme in 24 distinct plates. Before reading anything about WWI, students read this comic, react to it, and create questions about the war.

There is so much going on in this comic that students cannot possibly take it all in on the first viewing, and that's ok. I lay out two copies of the comic—one in the front and one in the back of the room—they span almost the entire width of the classroom. When the students come in, they are already talking about it and can't wait to find out more about it. I give the students a worksheet like the one for Nat Turner—they are tasked with writing a few sentences, connections, and questions on at least 12 of the 24 plates of the comic. The class is already divided into 7 small groups, and 2 will be reading/annotating the comic while the others are completing other reading work about WWI at their tables. At this point in the year, students are experts at visual literacy and finding specific visual evidence, and they immediately take to the assignment. I also have out WWI helmets, gas masks, and even a trench whistle—some will don the helmets or gas masks as they read the comic to really get into the assignment! Even though they are experts, the sheer amount of visual information in this comic is overwhelming, and this is the point—that we are not always going to notice everything on the first pass when reading. Often, we need to go back and re-read to fully understand what we are learning about. When the students share their worksheets, they are often surprised by what they missed but also at what they found. Students are always finding things that I did not notice before and making connections while also asking insightful questions. Many times, students will come back after school or pop in during lunch because they want to take another look at the comic. Now the students are hooked and want to learn more about WWI to answer their own questions.

Some sample student responses:

"Plate #24 made me realize how awful war was and how many soldiers risked their lives in battle. It seemed realistic since death counts were so high, which means each death was less meaningful as they were just buried so quickly."

"Plate 15 stuck out to me the most because it showed a soldier in the middle of cannon fire crying on his knees as if he just can't fathom what is going on."

"Plate 13—full of violence and explosions. It really captured and depicted the true violence and horror of war instead of glorifying fighting. A man was thrown in the air from an explosion, which was horrifying and insane. Also, the soldiers climbing out of the trenches shows their strength and courage."

"Plate #5—People were eating and I wondered what they could be eating and what they could be talking about. Also, if I could be on any one of those plates, it would be that one because I would rather eat than go to battle."

"I was surprised how long the battle lasted. In the tapestry comic, the battle went 2 days and 1 night. One thing I learned was how the layout of the trenches worked. I was able to see how the barbed wire and bags were used to fortify the trenches. The trenches also had wooden beams to support the ceiling of the underground bunkers. One thing that really stuck out to me was how many men were in the trenches and charged into no-man's land."

"The tapestry was extremely detailed . . . the scattered limbs reflected the uncertainty of surviving a charge outside the trenches. This tapestry taught me the value of establishing a network of entrenched positions and the dirty, cramped, and unpleasant conditions in the trenches."

"Is there a significance to the general walking by himself? Does it symbolize something?"

". . . the almost non-existent amount of space in some areas that weren't being bombed. Men were physically all cuddled up together, in craters, for protection."

"Why are there no women?"

"The soldiers with horses—were they the leaders? Ranked higher? Were they all Christian if they had the cross on their headstone?"

"Plate #6—on their way to fight and some of them had smiles on their faces and they didn't seem too serious. IF I was about to go into battle, I'd be terrified."

"It made me realized how much the war impacts the environment. Seeing the evolution of a place form a town to a graveyard actually is an important thing that this comic taught me. The plates of men running into no-man's land and being hit by open fire and mines takes the romanticism out of war. I was shocked."

"How long did the trenches take to make? Did people die while making them?"

We also read and annotate poetry from WWI, such as *Dulce et Decorum Est* from Wilfred Owens, and I notice students drawing visual representations of the poetry and their individual understandings of the words. Again, we may disagree over the meanings of certain lines, but that's ok—as long as we can explain and point to specific evidence. At the close of the WWI unit, students create their own original poetry, and they also create a visual that represents their prose. I am open to the format—some choose to create a comic, some a background image, others use the words themselves to create a powerful visual representation. I am always stunned by what the students create and love hanging them up in the hallway for all to enjoy. There are, of course, other elements to teaching about WWI, but these lessons form lasting mental images in the minds of students and serve as a more powerful assessment of learning than a traditional exam ever could.

Again, my classroom library is full of as many engaging topics and stories as I can find and full of books, both prose and graphic. I change out the book display to focus on books that correlate with each new unit of study. Overwhelmingly, it is comics that are picked up, read, and inspire further research and learning. One great example is *the Harlem Hellfighters* by Max Brooks and Caanan White, Broadway Books, 2014. Just the cover image alone is enough for a student, just walking by, to pick it up and become inspired to find out more.

11

Using Comics to Teach Essay Writing

Yep. You read that title correctly, essay writing through comics. As previously stated, I fully understand the need for all educators to focus on reading and writing, no matter the subject area. I also know that students can come to dread writing essays and research papers and often become overwhelmed. In 10th and 11th grades, and especially in college, we tend to have a certain expectation of writing skills from students, skills that they are expected to just know. However, in a content-heavy course, the writing skills can quickly become overshadowed by the vocabulary, names, etc. I know that I need to "cover" history from this time to this time, go over certain names, inventions, types of governments, etc. As a firm believer that students need to experience meaningful reading and writing in EVERY class, I always set aside time for just that, regardless of content time constraints. For our first formal writing response, I use a Star Wars comic that is written from the Stormtroopers' point of view—they are the good guys, if you will. This is *Star Wars #21*, September 2016, published by Marvel. (Jason Aaron writer, Jorge Molina artist, Matt Milla colorist, Chris Eliopoulos letterer.) I did buy a class set of this comic, but as with most, it can also be found in a digital format—$1.99 on Kindle and ComiXology at the time of writing. This lesson allows us to divorce content from skills in a fun, different, and engaging way. Once again, students enter the classroom, there are comics on the tables that they are not yet allowed to read, and the buzz begins.

The prompt for the essay is simple—are Stormtroopers good or evil? I have them first do some pre-writing and put down some quick ideas and examples. Not every student has a solid background in Star Wars (groan),

DOI: 10.4324/9781003291671-11

and this needs to be taken into account. These students can be allowed to do a quick google image search to get down some ideas. Once this is done, and we have had a chance to share out, students then read the comic, being told to pay attention to specific textual AND visual evidence to back up their writing. I tell them to keep an open mind, as one needs to when conducting research, and to not just look to prove their preconceived opinion. As researchers, we need to be able to change our minds when the evidence shows us a different path and not just try to pick the information that agrees with our original thesis/idea. The catch here is that students can ONLY use the evidence from the comic to answer the prompt—they cannot rely on their prior and sometimes extensive Star Wars knowledge. This forces the students to slow down and to really pay attention to the evidence. Often, the biggest Star Wars fans have the biggest initial struggle as they read and think, "Yeah, but. . . . "

As the comic is read and evidence is being collected, students fill out a T-chart with evidence of both good and evil traits of the Stormtroopers. Once completed, they then go through their lists to determine how they will prove their answer to the prompt, including a counter-argument. The T-chart is then used to create an MLA-style outline so that we can once again understand the importance of organization and pre-writing to create a cohesive and full argument. This minimum six-paragraph essay is then written and peer-reviewed. In a few days, I have opened the conversation on evidence-based essay writing, MLA formatting, counter arguments, thesis, outlining, and pre-writing. No matter what class they are in, they will be able to utilize these writing skills, as they will do later in our class. A crucial point for students here is that there is no one "right" answer to the prompt—just like in most questions. Students will not receive an "A" because they agree with my opinion, but rather through their use of evidence and persuasion.

A really fun part of the debriefing is when students pair/share the evidence that they found in the comic. Often, arguments will erupt between students centering on their differing views of the same image. This is the beauty of this lesson—that our personal viewpoints matter, that historians can look at the same artifact and yet reach different conclusions. This idea will be a thread throughout the school year as we often follow up answers with "why". Additionally, we analyze several images in the comic as tools of propaganda and why they work. Heroic pose is often used to portray the Stormtroopers, and this will help us to analyze propaganda-ridden images of Napoleon, Hitler, Stalin, and others later in the year. We also refer back to this comic when discussing viewpoint in the historic content through conflict—one person's hero is another's villain, one person's freedom fighter can be another's terrorist.

Of course, we can't just magically create analytical writers in high school and have to begin in the earliest of grade levels. For younger students, we can use the same type of lesson, just not culminating in a formal essay. We need to first begin with the skills of creating an argument, finding textual/visual evidence, and then organizing the information. I have found a lot of success in using *Frozen #1* (Joe Books, July 2016), written by Georgia Ball and illustrated by Benedetta Barone. After the events of the Frozen movie, Elsa and Anna are left as co-rulers in Arendelle, and everything seems to be working out well. However, when looking at different types of government, in this case, a sort of dual monarchy or even oligarchy, we know that each comes with its own advantages and pitfalls. Aside from the comic I use, the movies themselves could be analyzed for the same type of discussion—what might happen when a kingdom has two rulers and they disagree? Would it be better to have one strong ruler in control? Why or why not? Using this comic as an example, we see that there is an economic disagreement in the kingdom centering on land use between ox herders needing grassland to feed their animals for their coats and reindeer herders using the same land to cross these farms to get to the tundra, disturbing the ox farmland in the process. This disagreement ties into so many historical and economic topics—Manifest Destiny, pipeline construction, eminent domain, suburban sprawl, etc.! The comic depicts both sides as angry with one another, and their discussions end in loud disagreement with neither side willing or able to compromise. Elsa and Anna are both approached by one of the sides, and each makes promises without speaking to one another. The tension of the story results in many an angry face and almost erupts into violence. However, Elsa and Anna are able to get both sides together to discuss their mutual dependency on goods that they trade amongst one another and to eventual compromise. In this lesson, I stop the students from reading and ask them how, if they were either Elsa or Anna, how they would solve the problem on the next page, drawing their idea into a comic. We then look at how the issue was handled in the comic and compare our answers. The impact of this lesson was able to happen through the excitement and engagement of using a comic and well-known characters. However, the learning, divorced from heavy content, allowed students to dive deeply into important economic and government topics, while also discussing history and current issues. The students can then use this background to better understand future lessons on these topics. (I take back what I said at the beginning—this lesson would also be powerful in high school and even university level lessons! Imagine beginning an in-depth unit on political science and seeing the looks on the faces of 20-year-olds when you begin with a Frozen comic.)

12

Bringing Creators into Your Classroom, Being Human, Social Media, and the Emotional Impact of Comics

I am so thankful that AJ Juliani and Matt Heppe, two teaching colleagues, convinced me many years ago to share what I was doing on social media. At the time, I had little time for Facebook and had no idea what Twitter or Instagram even looked like. I really thought that it would be seen as bragging if I shared about my classroom on social media. These two colleagues really pushed me to share what I was doing, and I am forever grateful. However, it is through social media that I have been able to meet so many inspiring educators and creators. My advice to educators is not to be afraid to reach out to a creator and invite them into the classroom—especially in a virtual format. The worst they can do is say no, right? But when you reach out, be sure to talk about their work and to share how you use it in the classroom and how you can help get the word out about their inspiring work. While I have been blessed to have interacted with so many wonderful educators in this way, I am going to highlight one especially powerful meeting with a free online comic from ABC News and Marvel Comics. Before I get into the experience, go ahead and do a search for *"Madaya Mom"*. I'll wait.

This powerful comic came out in 2016, and I first heard about it when I was headed out to present at San Diego Comic Con. The Marvel booth was, of course, completely packed in all the floor chaos and giving out some really cool freebies. But I was only interested in one thing—getting a copy of this comic that I heard about—a comic telling the story of a mother in Syria just trying to help her family survive the ongoing conflict. I was able to get a hold of a single cherished copy, as not many were printed. I read it and

DOI: 10.4324/9781003291671-12

immediately knew that I needed to use it in my classroom. While Syria is not an official part of my curriculum, it is a vital place in history and current geo-politics. It is a place that is often in the news, but one which many Americans don't really pay attention to. Not only this, but the comic was also a primary source—the ABC News team of XANA O'NEILL and RYM MOMTAZ were able to use texts they received from a mother in Syria and approached Marvel to turn it into a comic! The amazingly talented Dalibor Talajic was chosen to bring these text messages to life in comic form. The website that accompanies this comic is another amazing resource with videos on how the comic was made, how the story was created, and so much more. First, I'll relate how I used the comic and then how we used social media to bring the team into our classroom.

When I first began as a teacher, the advice I was given was to not let the students see me smile until Christmas and to not divulge any personal information. Now that I am a, let's say experienced teacher, I realize how true it is to say only a Sith deals in absolutes. Over the years, I have allowed myself to be more flexible and to see my students as individual human beings—I also try to have them see me in the same way. Don't get me wrong, we can also go too far the other way by obliterating the line between teacher and student—there are parts of my personal life that will never be discussed with my students and, likewise, I would never ask from my students. That being said, forming relationships and realizing we are individuals goes a long way in creating a positive and productive classroom community—a community where vital and open conversations will happen respectfully.

Facebook is great for reminding us of what we did on a certain day throughout the years—it is often wonderful to see memories that have been posted. However, it can also remind us of a painful time, as can happen with family members and loved ones. My son, Liam, suffers from a rare form of Meningitis—so rare that we often need to explain it to medical professionals. We are lucky enough to live in the Philadelphia area with so many wonderful hospitals, doctors, nurses, etc. (we have been frequent customers at CHOP and St. Christopher's—have also traveled a bit south to visit the amazing Johns Hopkins) and to have solid health insurance (don't even get me started on the healthcare debate in our country). My son continues to suffer from migraines, body pain, and extreme fatigue and can even be hospitalized for days on end. He has undergone so many tests and evaluations, but the best prognosis we have been given is that he will hopefully grow out of it—we keep waiting, but it seems to be a life-long affliction. Facebook often shows me pictures of him in different hospitals over the years. He often has to miss out on so much with friends, and it can translate into struggles at school as well. As an example, we were at Camden Comic Con—it was a smaller convention on the campus of Rutgers University. We had taken a break and were sitting in a lobby (we always need to schedule breaks for my son on any trip so that he does not get too fatigued—this is what will lead to hospitalization) when he asked if he could sit in my lap. My first response was to tell him no—that he is too big to be sitting in my lap. But then I saw THAT look on his face—where I could tell he was in pain but wouldn't tell me. I quickly pulled him into my lap as I honestly just didn't care what any passing adult might think.

Other painful memories are of my father (my hero—a Philadelphia Cop), who suffered through ALS for about two years and was finally released in August several years ago. I had to watch this proud man suffer the wrath of a disease that continually shut down his body while keeping his mind 100% sharp and intact until the bitter end. He was the type of man who never wanted to rely on anyone or to ever ask for help—but he also had the most amazing sense of humor. It was so hard to watch him have to rely on me as our roles switched, and I took care of him. I won't get into much more detail here; I'll get to my point soon. My Dad died on the first day back to school, and I decided not to take any time off and just dedicated myself to my students and the all-important beginning of the year. The major turning point for me was sharing what happened and how my students were able to help me cope with this loss as we built a community that first week of school.

Here's my point, and one I make to my students. We are all human. We all struggle. We all need help and are often afraid to ask for it. There might be a reason why a teacher, or student, was snippy or short with someone. You never know what someone is going through as they come to school each day. I know so many teachers who are suffering through horrendous circumstances, yet they come to school every day with a smile and nothing but encouragement for their students. I also know that students come to school also dealing with serious issues. I have shared some of my experiences with my students, and they have with me as well. I see heroic deeds in front of me every day. I try to keep this in mind when a student has a "bad" day—I force myself take a breath and think about what is happening that has nothing to do with me. I am also a firm believer in restorative practices with my students—I truly believe that 99% of what happens in the day is never personal.

Oddly enough, perhaps, when President Trump ordered 59 missiles to be fired into Syria in April 2017, all of these thoughts came to mind, and I decided to scrap what I was doing on April 7 and to teach about the events in Syria. (I am a firm believer that teachers need to make connections to the real world, even if it is outside of the proscribed curriculum.) I knew that my high school students would have questions and that many would have heard different things—some true and some not. I also knew that some would fear a coming war and would have increased anxiety. However, as we were also preparing to learn about the Jewish Holocaust, I also thought this to be the perfect vehicle to discuss the false concept of "never again" and today's modern atrocities. I had *Madaya Mom* in mind to use at some point, and this was the perfect time.

When I looked through the teacher discussion guide on the comic's website, I came across the idea of asking students to reflect on a time in their lives when they felt powerless. This was the moment when my lesson plan completely came together. My Do Now was exactly that—think of a time in your life when you felt powerless and what steps you took to overcome it. The students then shared with their partners (we sit in collaborative tables of four), and I asked if anyone wanted to volunteer to the larger group. This was one of the only times that I did not walk around the room and interact with students as they worked on the Do Now—I did not want them to feel uncomfortable with my presence. I was astonished with what my students were willing to share and how much of a need for expression I had tapped into. I will not share their responses here to respect their privacy. I reacted to each volunteer, even taking the time to thank students for their bravery and to put my hand on their shoulder. Hugs even happened. I think I took them a bit by surprise when I shared my own times of feeling powerless—both as a father and a son. After speaking of my son, I related a particular time of powerlessness for me. He was given a spinal tap (one of several through the years) and was too young to be given a sedative. Four adults had to hold him down in the fetal position (I must admit a bit of pride there—strong lad!), and my job was to maintain eye contact with him and to talk with him so that he could be as relaxed as possible. I then told my students that I love them—that I do call them my kids and that I feel the same way when I see them struggle.

After this discussion, the students were all wondering why I had brought this all up—they know that I am notorious for making everything tie into academia, and this was no different. I told them that when I began teaching at 25, I thought I understood the Jewish Holocaust. I "knew" that all the Germans were evil and that I would have stood up and protected my Jewish students. But then I had kids. I now have a better understanding. No longer was life a simple choice for me—I now had to protect my own children. I would like to think that I would still be the outspoken fighter for justice—I just now understand that, to say the least, life is more complicated.

We then related all of this to a mother in Syria. A mother who had used social media in an attempt to get the world to help her family. To get the world to care. For me, 18 million dead in the African Holocaust, some 4 million in Holodomor, 6 million Jews, etc.—is just impossible to comprehend. I am a visual person, but photos of ghastly images cause the brain to shut down. But if I read about one person or one family—this personalization of history gets through to me in a profound way. *Madaya Mom* is a way to get this type of story and to make the events more accessible. I want my students to be able to relate to people in these events as, well, people. I want them to see them as normal people caught up in extraordinary events. I believe *Madaya Mom*, again, is an amazing way to make this happen.

My students were chomping at the bit during this entire introductory phase to talk about the missile launches into Syria—I had heard some asking each other why we weren't talking about it and were instead talking about our own lives in the Do Now. I finally explained what we were doing and turned them loose on the internet (we are a one-to-one laptop school) with some guided questions to find out about the civil war in Syria and why the United States was involved. The final question was one that pulled it all together—I asked the students to write down whether or not the US should send in more ground troops and to defend their reasoning. These types of culminating questions are so important—students should not only know how to research, but they should also understand the impact of world events on their own lives. They need to think for themselves and be able to defend their ways of thinking. This research was done on their own—I wanted to see what resources they used to find information. We had just spent several lessons researching fake news and source credibility—this was the perfect way to put this teaching to the test.

In 30 minutes, students were able to pair/share their responses and sources—I was impressed with their ability to gather a solid understanding of the history and current events in Syria. Some even made the Jewish Holocaust connection on their own and began to discuss. Next, we talked as a large group, looked at some maps, and discussed the impact of geo-politics on the region. We discussed Obama and Trump's choices in the region, the roles of the US and Russia and other players, etc.

For the next class, we read the *Madaya Mom* comic and watched videos from the accompanying website. Students were asked to create a document with the one panel in the comic that stood out the most to them. They then explained the meaning of the image and why they chose it—using specific textual (visual) evidence. The students chose so many different panels for a variety of reasons or chose the same image but interpreted it in different ways. It gave my students a chance to express their feelings, explore their perceptions, and listen to their peers. My hope is that exercises like these teach my students the value of looking more closely and hearing/seeing others while learning about a real-life event.

Afterwards, we focused on why this was made into a comic book—how we are a visual society, how it might help readers to connect, etc. Students were impressed that social media and text messaging were able to help get the word out about a struggling mother and her family. Again, the students were now emotionally and personally involved. We discussed how the text messages were being sent in Arabic—students had assumed that texts could only be sent in English. We were also able to discuss the breaking up of Yugoslavia and why Dalibor Talajic was chosen to draw the comic. In their reflections, students wrote about tearing up and becoming emotional due to Talajic's work (over and over, the students remarked about the powerful illustrations and how they were able to connect to Madaya Mom through them).

As part of the *Madaya Mom*'s online resources, Axel Alonso (editor-in-chief at Marvel) was interviewed in his office and discussed making the comic. That Marvel was willing to dedicate its considerable resources to help this mom was an inspiring moment for many students. Comics are not just capes and tights—we all know how comics are societal artifacts and can cause real change. This really brought together the core of my teaching and why comics are so important. Many comics tackle tough topics about our world today and are written on a deep and analytical level. As educators, we need to reinforce the power of this medium as another way to engage students in a meaningful and intelligent way. Superheroes truly are all around us, and Madaya Mom is certainly of them.

Amazingly, my students and I had the honor of Skyping with the authors, Xana and Rym, during one of the most powerful educational experiences I have ever had. My students arrived to class prepared with questions to ask, and the authors did not shy away from answering everything asked of them. I saw my students excitedly engaged in a personal way that would not have been possible through simply reading a textbook excerpt on Syria. One of the moments that sticks out to me the most is when Rym and Xana told my 10th graders how much of an impact this was having on them. That they were not sure that their work would have an impact, but after connecting with my students, they knew that Madaya Mom's story was making a difference. That she mattered. That their work mattered. When we debriefed after the session, my students were so impressed that these ABC News journalists were helped by us—that we had an impact on their lives. This is what happens when we open our classrooms beyond the four walls and make learning current and personal. It was mutually beneficial and a treat when we saw both Xana and Rym tweet out about their experience with us!

The *Madaya Mom* artist, Dalibor Talajic, also offered to share his experiences about the violent break-up of Yugoslavia. This was a powerful way for my students to not only understand how his emotions were translated into art and his connection with Madaya Mom, but also to better understand this important historical event and how it ties into modern genocide. Dalibor made the few sentences in our textbook come to life and made it personal for my students. In particular, he talked about tribalism and how it was a war of all against all—and how it is something that has happened time and time again in human history.

Lastly, I found an AMAZING Syrian-American Hip Hop artist who raps about Syria—Omar Offendum. I chose to share one of his songs, Crying Shame, with the class and handed out the lyrics before watching the video. We discussed some of the lyrics and their meaning before listening to the song. (I placed most of these lines in bold.) The students and I shared that this one song is something we should use at the beginning of the year to confront Western stereotypes about the Middle East and that this is a complicated issue. Through this one song, we were able to discuss culture (food, music, fashion), geography, refugees, geopolitics, and much more. There comes a time in the video when Offendum stops and looks directly at the camera and talks directly to the viewer in a powerful and compelling way. This makes the discussion personal and involves students on an emotional and individual level. The lyrics allow a powerful and engaging window into a world most of my students do not even know exists. We annotate a lot of songs in my class, and I often have students create their own songs to explain a time period, concept, etc. But—that's a different topic for another book. All of these skills came in reaction to a current event: my students were able to view a visual text, research, ask questions, interact with reporters and creators, make connections to digital, print, and lyrical texts, and walk away with a more complete and human connection to history. All this through "just" a comic.

Ultimately when we learned about WWII and genocide, I wanted my students to make connections to the modern impact of this war and the Cold War. I wanted them to see how one conflict hinges on and mirrors others—that while something like the break-up of Yugoslavia is an intricate and difficult to explain topic, it is one that needs to be researched, discussed, and learned. This is another example of humanity failing to learn the lesson of "Never Again" and that these events can happen anywhere. As we struggle with increased tribalism in the United States, I feel strongly that we need to reexamine the events in Yugoslavia and what can happen when we refuse to leave our own corners and ideologies. The world learned of "ethnic cleansing" what an insane word to use. Were we just trying to make ourselves feel better about yet another genocide? I fear, as Dalibor stated in his interview with my students, the idea of "everybody against everybody". I wanted my students to recognize and even feel the emotional impact of these events in Yugoslavia that are echoed in the *Madaya Mom* drawings because they are so powerful. Once again, I want my students to connect on a personal and emotional level with each other, with the text, and the world. As we later moved into learning about Yugoslavia, Dalibor was kind enough to offer to answer questions from my students about his experiences. I am moved beyond words at the offer, and now my students will again have an emotional and personal connection to important events.

Here are some student reflections from the close of this *Madaya Mom* lesson. Pay attention to their use of specific evidence. They are a good reminder of how we can empower our students to look at topics, at themselves, and their place in the world:

> This image made me feel some sort of responsibility for how helpless they are depicted. In the comic, most of the people's mouths are not even drawn. I take this to depict how they feel like they don't have any say/their words mean nothing. It makes me feel responsible for this because how I feel that I have to spread the awareness so the people in this picture, hopefully, will know that they are heard.

> It made me truly realize how much I love my family and that I would make any decision to save them from experiencing this kind of pain,

> The use of black creates a sense of darkness, isolation, and the scariness of the unknown. Splattered paint makes me imagine the mental/emotional state of the characters . . . 'They had to step in their friend's blood'—wow.

> This comic made me feel grateful for what I have in my life . . . one time, during a snowstorm, we lost all power—it was very cold at night even under all the blankets . . . my power was out only for a few days makes me feel horrible for this family.

> Panel #32—. . . throughout the comic, I felt teary-eyed and tried not to cry, but once I reached this panel, I hit a breaking point . . . it just shows Madaya Mom's hope deteriorating. Her goal is to keep her kids alive no matter what it takes, but at this moment, she says that 'death is more merciful than what they are going through now'

> Seeing them sleep together pulls at the heart strings as we connect with them as a family.

> This made me feel bad for the daughters because they look traumatized. The one girl on the left is clamping her fists together to show how angry she is. The other, however, looks as if she can't even hold herself together because she is leaning on her mother who is trying to calm the girls down.

> . . . Her sprawled position on the floor shows how helpless and weak she feels.

#3. We discussed the connection to the Battle of Stalingrad, Holodomor, German Hyperinflation from the 1920s, etc—all through the power of visualizations and how our minds connect to make meaning. The most obvious connection was to the Jewish Holocaust—this even led us to make a parallel to Anne Frank—what if she had a cell phone and social media? Could she have gotten out her story? Would anyone have cared? Would anything have been different?

This made me think of things that happen in the US—school shootings. I instantly thought of this because the panel has to do with girls watching their friends suffer from an event at school.

9/11 and the helplessness felt by the people in the buildings when they knew they were going to die.

I can connect as a lot of my family lives in Venezuela—not as bad as Syria, but—is currently going through a severe economic recession. There are protests that have been going on since 2014. Violence is at an all-time high. People can't earn enough money because of inflation to buy groceries or medicine.

13

Literature Adaptions

As a Reading Specialist, I understand the inherent ability of comics to engage readers of all levels. When choosing curricular resources, we can, of course, choose a graphic novel to use as a class set and central text. However, there are also many adaptations of prose books that can serve to enrich our readers and be available to help struggling readers, ELL readers, etc. as well. Having copies of these books can help by providing additional support and also enabling higher-level readers with more in-depth explorations. Just like with any adaptation, such as TV and film, some are good, and some just cannot be stomached by the lovers of the original. But even shortcomings can allow for powerful text-to-text discussions in the classroom as well as opportunities for students to really show their understanding of the material.

Additionally, graphic novel adaptations often allow for greater speed in reading and so can greatly benefit content area teachers, such as social studies, by allowing us to incorporate a complete text when there otherwise would not be time. These books can be used as a whole class reading or just be available for students to choose to read for further knowledge. One example from my own classroom is the manga version of Les Miserables, published by Manga Classics, edited by Stacy King, and drawn by TszMei Lee. I have several copies of the original in my classroom and do booktalk it, but few students have ever taken me up on reading the admittedly HUGE book. However, after showing clips from the movie and discussing the historical context, many students choose to borrow the manga adaptation that does contain much of the original wording. Although I have not used this as a

DOI: 10.4324/9781003291671-13

whole class resource, this could certainly be done as well. This allows students to be exposed to the original text and concepts of Hugo in the content area classroom, just in a much shorter time frame.

Many of my lessons circle back to the idea of individual interpretation, and a powerful tool in the classroom is to compare texts and mediums to one another. Text-to-text comparisons of graphic novels to prose are powerful ways to build this skill. Did the artist match your mental image? How would you have drawn it differently? How did the images change the meaning of a scene or character? In conversations with educators, some have expressed concerns that graphic novels take away the imagination of the reader as the story is literally depicted on the page. That, somehow, graphic novels are a lower level of reading as a result. However—as we have already seen in this book—much is also left to the imagination and for interpretation. These skills are highly transferable as students are able to quickly make connections between time periods and events/people.

One powerful example of a graphic adaptation is the one done for the twentieth anniversary of Laurie Halse Anderson's, *Speak*. This book means so much to so many, and, honestly, the graphic adaptation made me a bit nervous, wondering how the meaning would be honored. However, Emily Carroll, a talented artist, added depth and emotional power to the original prose through her black and white vivid imagery. My wife and I were hired by Macmillan publishers to write the educator's guide for this adaptation (full guide in the appendix). If you are somehow unfamiliar with this powerful book, *Speak* is a fictional story based on Laurie's own experience with rape in high school and is read in many schools. This is not just a story for girls—as it has much to teach all of us. I was able to understand Laurie's symbolism from the prose on an even more meaningful level through the illustrations. There is one image in particular (Images 13.1 and 13.2 Speak) that made me actually shut the book as it seared into my very soul. I am not overstating this idea, and it brought the story home to me in an emotional way. I suffered emotional and sexual abuse as a child, something I am only beginning to come to grips with as a 40-something-year-old. There has always been a beast in my guy, a gnawing animal of stress and anxiety that was always with me, just in varying degrees. When seeing this image, I immediately connected to the main character, Melinda, and saw myself in this story. And this is the power of comics—to connect in powerful ways and to see ourselves in these stories. I am not overstating when saying that this one image has helped me to begin coping with my own experiences as a child.

There is power in a visual form that allows for new exploration of familiar stories as well. For instance, there are many adaptations of Shakespeare's

Image 13.1 Speak
From SPEAK: THE GRAPHIC NOVEL by Laurie Halse Anderson; illustrations by Emily Carroll. Text copyright © 1999 by Laurie Halse Anderson. Pictures copyright © 2018 by Emily Carroll Reprinted by permission of Farrar Straus Giroux Books for Young Readers. All Rights Reserved.

Image 13.2 Speak
From SPEAK: THE GRAPHIC NOVEL by Laurie Halse Anderson; illustrations by Emily Carroll. Text copyright
© 1999 by Laurie Halse Anderson. Pictures copyright © 2018 by Emily Carroll Reprinted by permission of
Farrar Straus Giroux Books for Young Readers. All Rights Reserved.

Romeo and Juliet in many mediums. As many students read this story in schools, why not also offer a comic about Romeo and Juliet, set in a future with Montagues, cyborgs with manufactured DNA, and the Capulets, genetically enhanced humans, threatening to destroy the Empire of Verona while Romeo and Juliet, after falling in love, hope to bring about peace? *Romeo and Juliet: The War*, co-authored by none other than Stan Lee and published by 1821 Comics. My high school students read Romeo and Juliet, and I am absolutely not suggesting that we replace the original Shakespearean prose with this, well, awesomeness. But, don't we want students to think critically about how stories can be adapted and even modernized? How there are patterns in stories across cultures and time, not just from Shakespeare. Imagine students reading Romeo and Juliet and then being asked to reimagine the story in a different time or setting—to really show their understanding of the elements of the story. Another great option is *Romeo and Juliet (Shakespeare Classics Graphic Novels)*, by Gareth Hinds and published by Candlewick, which is a brilliant comics adaptation. In this faithful adaptation, Hinds creates a more universal and diverse cast of characters. Comics are wonderful for showcasing representation of peoples, and just seeing the cover is enough to get students thinking—Romeo and Juliet don't have to be white characters. This is an adaptation that has much of the original language but is abbreviated with occasional footnotes to explain some terms.

Still another wonderful way to support this unit is *Romeo and Juliet: the Graphic Novel*, adapted by John McDonald and illustrated by Will Volley, Jim Devlin, and Jim Campbell. There are different versions of this book—Original Text, Plain Text (translated into modern English), and Quick Text (an abbreviated version with modern prose). The absolutely brilliant aspect of these books is that the images are EXACTLY the same, no matter what version of prose is being used. This immediately opens the ability to adapt to individual reader needs without making it easy for other students to discern what version others are reading, thus allowing for privacy and increased confidence. Whatever your classic or core text, I encourage you to look for different graphic versions- to consider how they remain true to the text and to explore how they are different. And if one does not exist- consider having your students create one! (Images 13.3 and 13.4 Romeo and Juliette Quick Text).

As I have said before, comics are wonderful for all levels of students, and Advanced Placement (AP) courses are not different. I remember struggling through reading the Communist Manifesto in my Western Civilization course in college. When I taught AP European History, I also wanted to expose my students to reading this short, but impactful, book. Of course, we also read Adam Smith and many varying political/economic theories as well. But, how

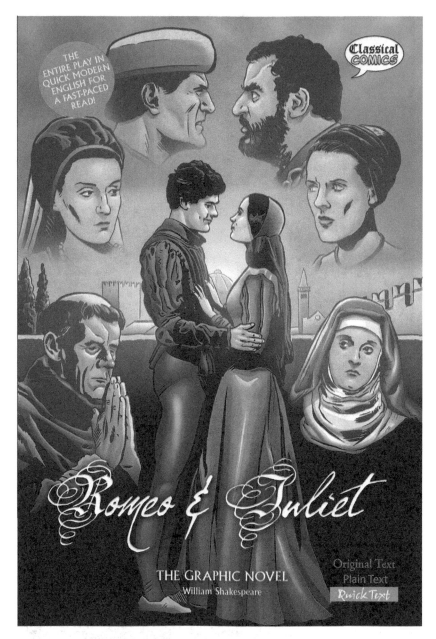

Image 13.3 Romeo and Juliette Quick Text

Romeo and Juliette Quick Text © Classical Comics www.classicalcomics.com
Romeo & Juliet The Graphic Novel: Quick Text Version
ISBN: 978-1-906332-21-1
Publisher: Classical Comics
Script Adaptation: John McDonald
Character Designs & Original Artwork: Will Volley
Colouring: Jim Devlin
Lettering: Jim Campbell.

Image 13.4 Romeo and Juliette Quick Text

Romeo and Juliette Quick Text © Classical Comics www.classicalcomics.com
Romeo & Juliet The Graphic Novel: Quick Text Version
ISBN: 978-1-906332-21-1
Publisher: Classical Comics
Script Adaptation: John McDonald
Character Designs & Original Artwork: Will Volley
Colouring: Jim Devlin
Lettering: Jim Campbell

could I best help 10th-grade students navigate a text as dense as the Communist Manifesto? How could I get them excited to read it and not falter in frustration? Luckily, I came across the work of Fred Van Lente and Ryan Dunlavey—their impressive *The More than Complete Action Philosophers*. This comic could be used as a central text for a course in philosophy—beginning with Lao Tzu and ending with Jacques Derrida. Not only does their work showcase the ability of comics to be intelligent and engaging, but it also proves to be the perfect intro for my AP Euro class (Image 13.5 Marx). We were able to build needed background knowledge BEFORE reading the dense text in a fun and meaningful way. The concepts we needed to understand were challenging to visualize until *Action Philosophers* literally allowed my students to form concrete mental images of these concepts, thus making the prose easier to grasp. As a window into what we were able to learn, here are just some of the questions my students were able to answer.

What creates value in a commodity?
How can the proletariat free itself from bourgeoisie domination?
How did Marx modify Hegel's dialectic theory?
Why does Marx not approve of capitulation to capitalism?
Why have capitalists moved into the Third World?
In three sentences, explain why milk is cheaper than gold.

By using the visual text to accompany the prose text, my students were able to better navigate, question, and analyze the dense material. It gave them a sense of accomplishment and a better understanding than simply googling answers. It helped ease the reading of the actual text by building background knowledge in a fun, engaging way.

Another adaptation I used in my AP Euro course, and also 10th grade Global Studies, is *The Plot—the Secret Story of the Protocols of the Elders of Zion* by Will Eisner. This anti-Semitic fictional document, presented to the world as fact, supposedly details the Jewish plot to take over the world. In comic form, the work of Eisner allows students to see the impact of this on world history and current events. By the end of the lesson, we are having a powerful discussion on media literacy, historiography, and more. Some of the questions we answer:

1. Will Eisner stated a specific reason for creating this book. What was it? (In the Foreword)
2. Briefly explain three reasons why Russia was ripe for this "document" to be published.
3. What were two of the reasons given how people would be duped?

Image 13.5 Marx—Van Lente and Dunlavey
Ryan Dunlavey art, Fred Van Lente author Evil Twin Comics (November 11, 2009)

4. How was the forgery carried out? How did it get into the hands of the public?
5. Cite evidence explaining its falsity. Explain.
6. How/why did Hitler use this "document"?
7. How did the events surrounding the Dreyfus Affair impact the creation of this "document"?
8. Overall opinion? What did you think of this document? How has it impacted you?

As teachers, we are always looking for ways to make difficult topics accessible and to help the students go deeper into their own analysis. Being open to using graphic interpretations like these is invaluable in fostering meaningful conversations.

I can't emphasize enough that there are so many graphic options available for all levels, subjects, and perspectives. In my own classroom, I look for a wide range of interests, authors, and depictions. For example, sometimes Science Fiction can be overlooked in the Language Arts curriculum, and even when included, books can often center on white male characters and authors. However, Damian Duffy and John Jennings create two wonderfully insightful adaptations of Octavia E. Butler's prose novels. *Parable of the Sower* was published in 2020, and *Kindred* was published in 2018, both by Abrams. There is so much to unpack in these adaptations, and they could be used in multiple courses—social studies, Language Arts, psychology, philosophy, etc. *Kindred* opens the door to powerful discussions centering on the what if of time travel, of history, of treatment of women in such a way that the reader feels as though they are pulled into the story. Through the story-telling and compelling imagery, I know that I personally felt part of these horrific events and that they would lend themselves to not just discussing the historical context, but the why's and how's of society that lead to this story.

Excitingly, we are also seeing graphic adaptations of more current books, such as *the Crossover* by Kwame Alexander and adapted by Dawud Anyabwile and *Long Way Down* by Jason Reynolds and adapted by Danica Novgorodoff. There is even an upcoming adaptation of Ibram X. Kendi's *Stamped from the Beginning: The Definitive History of Racist Ideas in America*, illustrated by Joel Christian Gill and to be published by Ten Speed Press in 2023. These provide invaluable opportunities to pair current prose titles with current graphic titles- to assist students with visualization, with comparison, with learning difficulties, or to just slow down and go deeper into the meaning beneath the story. They also allow us to reach readers where they are.

Whatever you teach, there are so many wonderful comic adaptations in the world, and it would be impossible to list all my favorites. Just like with movie and TV adaptations, some graphic adaptations work better than others, some are more faithful to the original than others, but regardless they help us to build those crucial analytical skills through text-to-text comparisons. There are some titles that I would not use in their entirety, but I will share with students a few panels to open discussion about what works and what doesn't. If the adaptation doesn't work, students can reimagine their own version in either comic form! And, if a graphic version does not exist, I might have my students create one for a chapter or a scene. One such way is when my students read *Frankenstein* by Mary Shelley in their Language Arts class and I give them the historical context of the time period and how it may have impacted the author's creation of this story. I ask my students to imagine what the monster of today would be—what is it that we are afraid of in society? They used symbolism to create their monster and draw either one illustration or as many panels as they want in comic form. Students have created children zombified by their cell phones, "monsters" that are transgender, Muslim immigrants, and many other examples. Wow—the in-depth conversations we have really showcase the deep and meaningful conversations we have around society and the fear of the "unknown". This short activity brings depth and meaning to a classic text and allows students to connect it to their world.

14

Fairy Tales and Folk Tales as Artifact

There are times in courses when the content becomes a bit "dry" and tough to teach, or even just overloaded with content jargon. I experience this when I begin the unit that focuses on how feelings of nationalism led to the unification and creation of Germany. I struggled with connecting this idea and highlighting its importance. I wondered how I could best help students to understand how culture can help a people come together (and also tear it apart). It's really tough in the United States, as our wondrous diversity makes it challenging to point to truly universal American culture. In reading through our Global History textbook, I saw a brief mention of the Brothers Grimm. What's so important about folk tales? This thought stuck in the back of my head and came back when I was perusing the sale bins at a local bookstore and found two books on the Grimm collected stories: The *Illustrated Grimms' Fairy Tales: Eight sinister tales from the Brothers Grimm* (Literary Pop Up), Canterbury Classics 2013. Not only did this book have the original (terrifying) stories, but there were also several pop-ups that were just awesome. I immediately bought 7 copies of the book, one for each table of students. I then found *The Big Book of Grimm*, Jonathan Vankin author. This book is a collection of some lesser-known and all of the well-known stories, but wonderfully illustrated and published by DC Comics! Again, I bought several copies, and my mind began to lesson plan right there in the bookstore. What I found reading the books surprised me, as I realized that the current "Disneyfied" versions of the stories were often quite different from the originals. I asked myself why these stories had changed and what these changes revealed about the societies

DOI: 10.4324/9781003291671-14

in which they were written? These are questions I wanted my students to explore. I decided to have my students read the stories and tell me what they thought was being revealed. I first did this lesson in my AP European History course, but now use it on multiple other levels as well.

Students are always curious, and a bit excited, when they come into the classroom and see materials on the desk—especially pop-up books and comics. As I now have copies of each book for students, I ask them to discuss what stories they want to read at each table—it really doesn't matter which one they choose, as long as they don't repeat one another. They then answer the following four questions:

1. What do you know about the story already (before reading)—give a general summary.
2. What was different in the account you read?
3. What insight does the original story give to the society in which it was written? What is the moral?
4. What insight does the modified (modern) version give about the society in which it was written? Why has it been changed?

Once again, pop culture offers a powerful window into society, and these four questions lead to insightful and animated conversations. Students can't wait to share about what they read, such as the hacking off of heels and toes to fit into glass slippers. . . . We discuss US society and the idea that adolescence continues to age 25, what it means to be a child, and how that concept has changed over time. Why were these original stories told? Were they just stories to sell amusement park tickets? Or were children told these stories for their own good? How could they unite a people? We let the conversation go where it goes, often getting into nursery rhymes, such as Ring Around a Rosie and its connection to the Bubonic Plague. We have also discussed Bloody Mary (Mary Tudor) and why this story was created (to remind the English of the apparent dangers of having another Catholic monarch—children would not forget when they became adults). So many students relate late-night, sleep-over terrors of seeing this creature in a bathroom mirror while having no idea that this was based on a real person!

We then widen the lens to research tales from cultures around the world as we look for similarities and patterns. https://fairytalez.com/ is a great resource of free tales from around the world. We even found a great resource on Google Earth from Literacy Central, titled Fairy Tales From Around the World. In this activity, students can click on different regions around the world and explore different tales. I also raided the bookshelves of my own children and brought in print books while remaining on the lookout for books in the children's section of bookstores. Another source can be the old Fractured Fairy Tales cartoons from my youth—widely available on YouTube. These show how tales can be changed. Finally, never underestimate the power of asking students about tales that they were told in their childhood or to even go home and ask family members.

Once students have read, reflected upon, and discussed multiple tales, they then create their own and depict them in comic book form (more of how to create comics in Chapter 16). Students can choose to use an online comic creation tool, such as Pixton Edu, or can hand draw them—or use a combination of the two. When assigning the comics to be created, I also supply several types of blank comic book pages that students can choose to use as a template because sometimes a blank page can overwhelm students. I purposefully leave the assignment open as to materials and expectations—the criteria are just that it must be a moral tale, have a minimum number of panels, and be a complete story with some sort of "fantastical" element. The students are encouraged to put a modern twist on a classic tale, but they can also create their own original story as well. Because I have a classroom that is full of representation of both character and creators, my students often feel safe creating stories that represent themselves. I have cried reading some of these stories as I know my students and who they are. There are stories about being transgender, coming out, pushing back against racism, and so much more. Of course, there are also the stories that are just silly fun, and that is perfectly awesome as well!

Once the students have completed their comics, they pair/share at their small tables. I cannot explain enough how impactful these groupings of four students are as they become a small family. They feel comfortable with one another and support one another. In fact, when I offer to change up the seating chart later in the year, I am most often met with a resounding no. I ask if anyone wants to either share their own story or that of a partner. They can choose to read the story and/or to show the art. If a student is nominated by another and does not want to present, we immediately move on with absolutely no pressure. Once this is completed, students then walk around the room, reading and discussing the work of other students. They rank their top 3 comics with a short explanation of their choices. We then take the top comics from all five of my classes and put them onto an online voting form (Google works well). I also often add in a favorite few of my own—teacher's privilege! There are no names attached to the comics. We then send the form out to the entire district to vote, and I also share out on social media. We have even had the PA Secretary of Education voting for his favorite as well! Ah— the power of social media and breaking down the walls of the classroom (Image 14.1 Teagan Smyth).

Image 14.1 Teagan Smyth
Teagan Smyth @TeagsWorld

I love this lesson. It was inspired by content that I found a bit dry and unimportant because I did not initially see its value. This content was just a few sentences in the textbook and often completely overlooked. However, after making connections to my own love of pop culture and story-telling, this became a multi-day lesson, which I personally enjoyed. We were able to not only understand this historical content, but also to make connections to today and to further build class community.

15

Civil Rights

The number one question I am always asked: "Who is your favorite superhero or comic?" For me, it's an easy and immediate answer—Congressman John Lewis and the *March* graphic novel trilogy by John Lewis, Andrew Aydin, and Nate Powell. As I wrote in an article for PBS NewsHour Extra, "There is no better superhero—fictional or not." I am moved to tears each time he speaks about the love and forgiveness in his heart, despite what he suffered through. My own kids were lucky enough to have shaken his hand during a signing at San Diego Comic Con. I pattern many of my decisions on Lewis' life and message—that of getting into trouble, good trouble. Necessary trouble. His message for students is we need to get involved and not idly watch bad things happen. Like the students in SNCC (Student Non-Violent Coordinating Committee), young people can be a meaningful force for change in this world."

These three books are the most powerful teaching resources I have ever used in my 20 plus years of teaching. We are able to learn not just about THE civil rights movements, but also to see a much wider picture of the movement, its history, and the continuing struggle for equality and respect for all. Students are able to see beyond the towering figures of Martin Luther King, Jr. and Rosa Parks. They feel personally responsible through the powerful illustrations. They want to learn more. Some students have even told me that this is the first book they have honestly read cover to cover. The days we are reading these books are my favorites of the year, and I am always sad when we are finished and I put the books back into the closet, waiting to open more

DOI: 10.4324/9781003291671-15

minds again the following school year. I will give a summary of how we use these books here, but there are also more detailed lessons in the appendix.

Before reading *March* Book 1, we read the *Martin Luther King and the Montgomery Story* comic—this artifact was published in 1957 and distributed by the Fellowship of Reconciliation (FOR) and was edited in part by King himself! This is not the only comic published during the movement, but it is the one we use to begin our learning. This comic was intended to inspire young people and teach about the tenets of non-violence. People of all ages read and were inspired by this comic, including a young John Lewis. Co-author of *March*, and Digital Director/Policy Advisor for the congressman, Andrew Aydin is largely responsible for bringing this comic back into the public's knowledge after learning about it from Lewis. I love the historical connection between the impact of this comic on Lewis and how the *March* Trilogy is now inspiring young people today. When reading the comic, not only are students learning about the Montgomery Bus Boycott and the power of this action, they are also learning how to read a comic before getting into the more in-depth trilogy.

While I could write entire chapters about teaching with these powerful resources, I will share just a few examples about how to use it, but there are even more resources on my website (TeachingWithComics.com). When I first taught *March*, I was somewhat under pressure to showcase the efficacy of using graphic novels in the classroom as it was the first district purchased comics resource. I wanted students to get the most out of *March* Book 1 and so created a rather lengthy guided reading packet, asking for specific textual/visual evidence, question making, personal reflections, and even points where we stopped to draw and summarize. *March* Book 1 is the shortest of the three and a perfect chance to really get into the skills of annotating and reading a comic. We, as usual, pair/share reactions and debate the meanings of the illustrations. I show some sample panels on the board, and we analyze them together. I was fully prepared to write similar guided reading packets for the other two books, to ensure that students were reading and understanding the history. However, I noticed that students were often stopping in their reading because they could not wait to share their reactions with one another. In fact, students asked that we dedicate more time in class to reading the books and not read them for homework as they really loved sharing their observations with one another. This was not a mere ploy to get out of homework as I saw the students excitedly coming into class ready to read and discuss.

For *March* Book 2, following these observations, I gave a more general packet—one that asked students to summarize groupings of pages while still writing down some reflections and questions. However, I saw that the packet was getting in the way of their honest enjoyment from reading this powerful book and which led me to take a risk with book 3. I knew that, when I read the March Trilogy, I was not taking copious notes, but rather reading with sticky notes and putting them in the pages where they fit—reflections, questions, important moments to discuss. My books are always marked up—I can't read without a highlighter and sticky notes at the ready. So, I went and amassed a large collection of sticky notes and handed them out to my students, along with Book 3. My only directions were to read and place a sticky note when students were moved to do so. We brainstormed and discussed what should be written on these notes and when they should be placed. I was a little nervous—there was no minimum given, no rubric, no direct evidence of learning I could point to if my administration asked for it. (This was a pressure I put on myself—my administration has always been very supportive and encouraging when it comes to risk-taking in the classroom.) That being said, I handed out the books and sticky notes, sat in my chair with the same, put my feet up on the desk, and began to read with the students. (I have taught these books many times, but I always read them again with the students. I put everything else aside—I do not grade, I do not open my laptop.) My room has comfy chairs around the room to read in, and I encourage students to move about and get comfortable when reading. Some choose to put in earbuds, some choose to eat, but everyone reads.

This lesson, this simple "plan", is an amazing experience. Students talk to one another when they are moved to do so. I take a break from my own reading and walk around the room from time to time, and students routinely ask me to sit down with them so they can share a moment in the book with me. At the beginning of each new class, we take a few moments to pair/share and large group share where we are placing sticky notes. There is some concern from students that they may not be putting in enough or that they are missing information that others picked up on. As we share, though, students often show that they have a simple question mark next to a specific panel or an exclamation point (sometimes even "WTF!" is written). Other times, students are moved to place several sticky notes on the same page as they want to write more in-depth, reflect, and make personal connections. At the end of reading book 3, I take a lot of time to read through each of these books, now tripled in size from all the sticky notes, and to write a summary based on their reflections. It really is that simple when you have a powerful resource to use in the classroom.

The amazing thing is that we personally get to know John Lewis and those around him in the movement. Of course, my students learn about the facts and the towering figures, but we also move beyond this to realize that movements are made up of individuals—that we can all have an impact on the world around us. Some students have even made signs for the classroom—images of John Lewis with the words "what would John do?" that serve as a reminder that we can all make a difference. Through this process, the Civil Rights Movement becomes humanized and accessible, relevant, and impactful. The sneaky part of all this is that students have also become deeper readers as they have annotated text in deep and meaningful ways on a personal level. This becomes the foundation for another assignment where students consider and defend the current civil rights movements they see in the world. This will be discussed in a later chapter on making comics.

Another notable text on this topic is *La Voz De M.A.Y.O: TATA RAMBO* by Henry Barajas and J. Gonzo, Image Comics 2019. It provides a wider view of the Civil Rights movement, as it collides with journalism, historiography, and family story-telling. The author, Henry Barajas, is the great-grandson of Ramon Jaurigue, an integral civil rights leader who co-founded the Mexican, American, Yaqui, and Others (M.A.Y.O.) organization, helping the Pascua Yaqui tribe achieve federal recognition and rights. It is impossible to teach every important topic and person in a social studies class, but comics like these better enable us to include variety and depth in our classrooms. I had not heard of Ramon Jaurigue before reading this comic, but I came away fully impressed, not only with his heroic efforts, but also with the way this book was constructed. Barajas amassed many primary sources, including oral histories and newspaper articles, and included them in the comic as he shared his process. This inspired me to write a teacher guide for this comic, which is included in the appendix.

Another possible way to teach civil rights is to show students how fiction can be used to bring awareness to difficult events. There is an excellent example of this also from Andrew Aydin, co-author of the March Trilogy and Run. In *Marvel Comics Presents #3*, May 2019 (artwork by Daniel Acuna and lettering by Joe Caramagna), Aydin wrote a story placing Captain America in 1964 segregated Mississippi. As Cap mysteriously crash lands into the story, he winds up protecting a Black family who helped nurse him back to health. As a white superhero, Cap thinks he best knows how to help this family protect themselves from some angry white people who are trying to keep Blacks from voting and fighting for equality. However, he discovers that it's not as easy as punching one's way to equality and that it will take much longer than just one fight. As we learned in the March Trilogy, there are organizations, such as CORE, COFO, and SNCC, that are in the background helping with this fight. As the story progresses, students can discuss how Cap has a hard time reconciling that he is the symbol of an America that does this to its own citizens. This is a powerful and emotional fictional story that lends weight to comics as a medium for expressing societal issues, but it also shows well the sometimes overlooked power and place of using historical fiction in the classroom.

I was thrilled to see that the March Trilogy has been continued with the graphic novel titled *Run*—Congressman John Lewis and Andrew Aydin co-authors, L. Fury and Nate Powell art (published by Abrams Comicarts, 2021). As of the writing of this book, I have not yet had the opportunity to teach with Run, but I will be doing so in the near future. This book continues to follow the life of John Lewis and his efforts to bring civil rights to every American. I chose to share four of the images here to showcase the power of comics in our classrooms. On page 4, we once again see the emotional and terrifying confrontation between Lewis and those enforcing the law in an unequal way. We can see the difference in body language between the police and protestors and the looks in the eyes of the protestors. By looking at the words chosen to be in bold and the shapes of the word balloons, the reader can immediately sense the tension as the scene unfolds. I know that my students will once again notice the bystander bringing a child to watch the goings-on as they wonder where that child is today. On page 23, we see the struggle to simply vote become real as we notice hooded KKK members standing next to law enforcement. We see the sweat and worry on the face of those trying to register to vote. This scene is chilling and makes real the danger inherent in just trying to exercise one's right to vote. On page 40, we see images that allow us to make powerful connections between two events many students do not see connected. Too often, we teach about the Vietnam War in one chapter and the Civil Rights Movement in another, but we need to help students see their interconnectedness. The fast-paced images here allow us to do just that in a powerful way that students will remember, that they will internalize in a personal way (Images 15.1–15.4 Run).

Civil Rights, past and present, are an ongoing topic included in many of our curriculums. I have found that by providing a variety of choices, students will readily choose comics that appeal to them and then are inspired to conduct further research on their own. More than that, by focusing on individuals and on depth, our students learn that the journey to a more perfect union is not always easy, relies on communication and endurance, and is the quest for all individuals to be seen as equals.

Image 15.1 RUN

From RUN by John Lewis, Andrew Aydin, L. Fury, and Nate Powell. Copyright © 2021 John Lewis and Andrew Aydin. Used by permission of Abrams ComicArts™. Harry N. Abrams, Inc., New York. All rights reserved.

Image 15.2 RUN

From RUN by John Lewis, Andrew Aydin, L. Fury, and Nate Powell. Copyright © 2021 John Lewis and Andrew Aydin. Used by permission of Abrams ComicArts™. Harry N. Abrams, Inc., New York. All rights reserved.

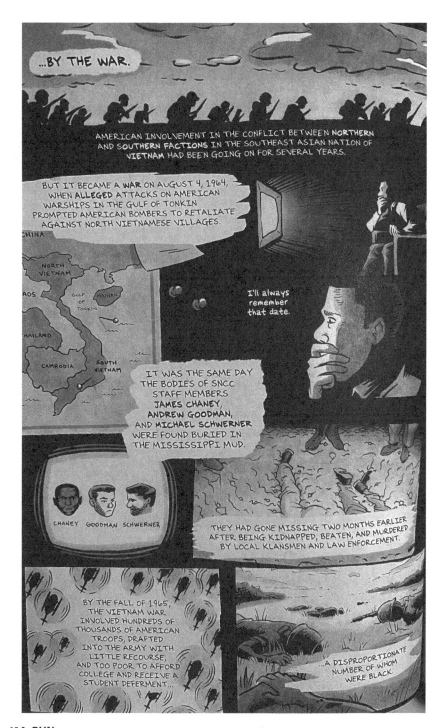

Image 15.3 RUN

From RUN by John Lewis, Andrew Aydin, L. Fury, and Nate Powell. Copyright © 2021 John Lewis and Andrew Aydin. Used by permission of Abrams ComicArts™. Harry N. Abrams, Inc., New York. All rights reserved.

Image 15.4 RUN

From RUN by John Lewis, Andrew Aydin, L. Fury, and Nate Powell. Copyright © 2021 John Lewis and Andrew Aydin. Used by permission of Abrams ComicArts™. Harry N. Abrams, Inc., New York. All rights reserved.

16
Making Comics

Making comics is an engaging and often unique experience for students and a way to involve students with different talents. Making a comic forces students to think deeply, research, pre-write, edit, and so much more. There are so many applications for making comics in all classrooms that the lesson ideas are almost endless. I have already shared a few lessons where students made comics in my classroom, and this section will focus more specifically on how to do so. Your comic-making session could occur in one class period or span several weeks—it all depends on what is needed. The first step, though, is to discuss the many roles that go into making a comic, as well as the assurance that a student doesn't need to be a celebrated artist in order to tell their story. Once done, students can be placed into groups and roles assigned according to their strengths—artist, colorist, letterer, researcher, story-boarder, etc.

The most powerful lesson in my class is when the students complete the *March* Trilogy. Students are then tasked with finding a modern civil rights issue of their choosing, after conducting some initial research. This really does open quite a few minds to the idea that the movement did not end in the 60s and that there are many civil rights issues that continue today—access to education and health care, LGTBQIA+, women, minority, physically and mentally handicapped, etc. We then begin sharing the initial research and deciding which ones to turn into comics. I leave it open to the students—that they can work alone, in pairs, or up to five students in a group. They have to pitch to me their topic, what each student will be doing in the groups, and why so many are needed. We then begin the research process with students

DOI: 10.4324/9781003291671-16

keeping track of credible sources (we establish this all-important skill in the beginning of school), citations, specific information, etc. Next, students brainstorm and create sketches/storyboards. As I check in with each group, I look for their completed storyboards/outline before giving the go-ahead to begin making the comic. The comic is created over the course of 4–5 class periods. I do have several ironclad expectations from students:

> Specific evidence presented at least once on each page—with a footnote giving proper citation to the source (we use MLA). This can include statistics, quotes, etc.
> Annotated works cited page with a minimum requirement of sources.
> A minimum number of panels.
> A cover of the book with a "catchy" title, an image to draw in the reader, and the names of the group members, just like we see on many comic book covers.
> On the back, there is a summary of the story and the group names again, this time with their role in making the comic.
> This needs to be a complete story and must have a potential and realistic solution to the issue.

Once completed, we share between the classes, and each group presents their comic to be read in digital format. Students WANT to read one another's comics, and we have in-depth conversations that often refer back to John Lewis and the 60s while students make connections to today. Through this sharing, students learn about many of the issues currently facing us, but in a way that I could not have accomplished simply by having them read news articles, etc. While the time commitment to creating these comics is a bit on the high side, the pay-off is at the end when we discuss so many vital topics in a relatively short amount of time. Each time, without me needing to start the conversation, students begin brainstorming ways that they can help solve these real-life issues as researched and depicted in their comics. In doing so, it allows students to show passion and interest in their own topics while also respecting and listening to the viewpoints about topics their peers feel strongly about as well. At the end of the lesson, my students have researched, analyzed, cited, presented, debated, discussed, and learned. The time is well worth the experience and skill-building.

How do we create the comics? Many students, even the talented artists, are initially squeamish about sharing their artwork. Many tell me that they can't draw. I know that I first need to explain that I am not grading on artistic ability here—that it is about the story-telling and that there are many ways to accomplish this task. We brainstorm different mediums and how they can be used to tell a story in a comics format. Below are just some possibilities, but I am also open to student ideas and suggestions on how they can make the comic.

> **Hand draw**—the time commitment to this cannot be overstated and needs to be openly discussed with students. Too many times, the group just expects the artist in the group to put in a lot of extra time to create the illustrations, and this can cause a lot of pressure. One way around this is to have the artist create the front and back covers of the comic and to use other methods for the interior (see below). There are times when an artist really wants to create the entire comic, and I do allow this after meeting one on one with the student to discuss whether their plan is feasible and practical in the time given.
>
> **Hand draw using the computer**. My own kids love to use the iPad and touchscreen laptop with the Procreate app. There are many different ways to do this. Don't forget to reach out to the art department—we are often borrowing drawing pads for the computers.
>
> **Photographs**—students can take their own photos (or ones from free image sources) and put them into a comics format. Students can also use historical photographs with proper citations given. The simplest way to do this is to upload into PowerPoint where students can create dialogue balloons (insert, shapes, callouts) in the images to tell the story. They can also put in colored text boxes to create a narrator's block.
>
> **Toys**—I have had students tell the story using Lego figures and other toys. They can then take pictures and create their comic.
>
> **PowerPoint**—my daughter used the draw feature in PowerPoint, along with a stylus, to create an ongoing crafting book in a comic book style! (Images 16.1–16.4).
>
> **Pixton**—I love the use of Pixton in class when making comics. There are other online tools, but I have found this one to be the easiest to use. My daughter used this to make comics for her fifth-grade class; at the latest count, she is up to 150 pages! (Images 16.5–16.8).

One wonderful resource motivating students in the comics creation process, and story-telling in general, is through the use of Jarrett Lerner's inspiring resources. He understands the initial hesitancy students experience when facing a blank page. Through his activities, students gain the confidence to tell their own stores. Although these resources are geared more towards younger students, I also use them in my high school to take away the anxiety and focus on the story-telling (Images 16.1–16.9 Jarrett Lerner). Jarrett shares a lot of

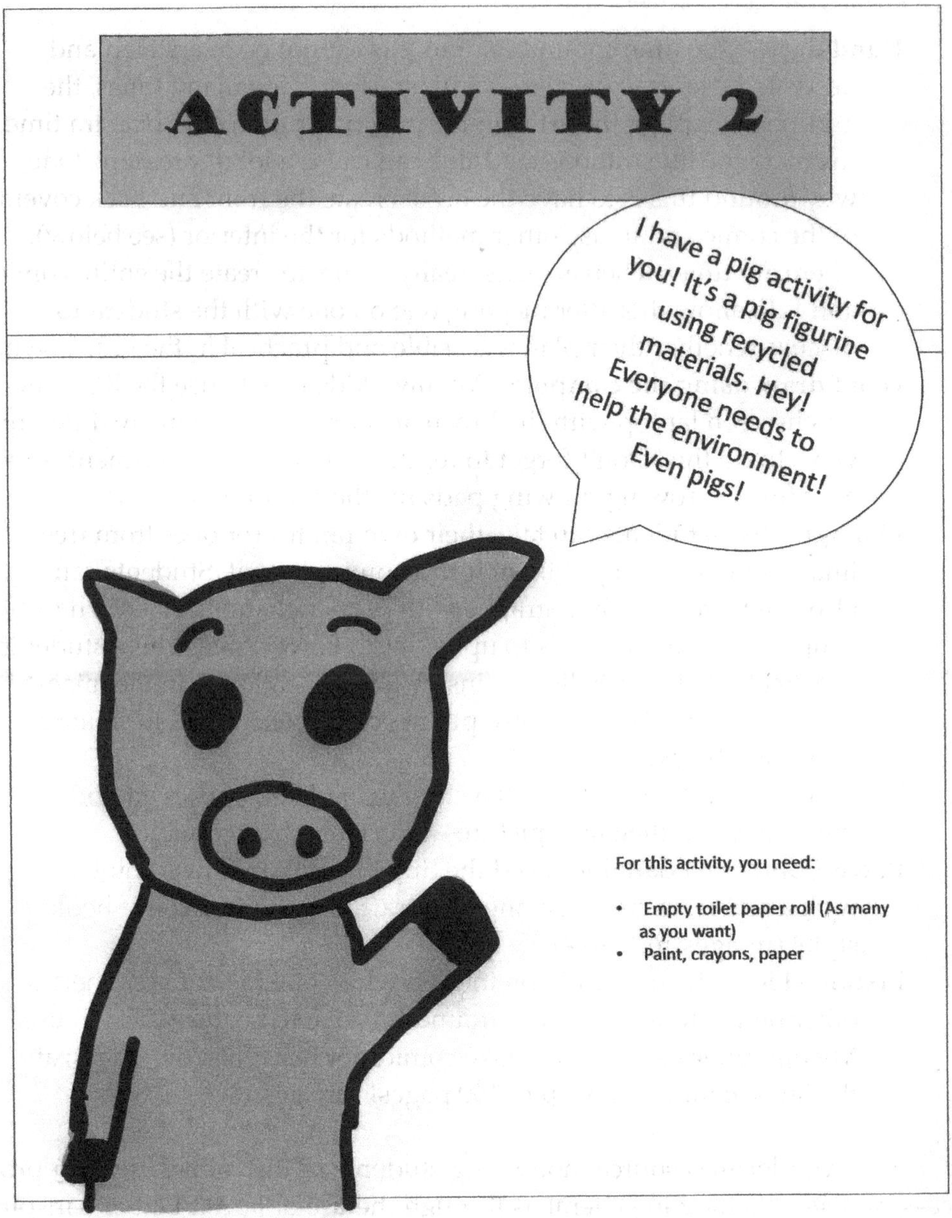

Image 16.1 Teagan Smyth
Teagan Smyth @TeagsWorld

For this activity, you will be creating ME! The goal is to create a cute pig stuffed animal! Also, if you don't want to follow the directions fully, and you want to make it your own, you are completely welcome to!

Materials:
Pink felt
Black felt
Scissors
Needle & Thread (Ask your parent's permission for the needle first!)
Stuffing of some sort (Newspaper, Standard Stuffing, Extra felt, or anything you think would work!)

Image 16.2 **Teagan Smyth**
Teagan Smyth @TeagsWorld

Image 16.3 Teagan Smyth
Teagan Smyth @TeagsWorld

1. Draw the outline of a pig's body on the felt. Don't draw the tail, we'll add it on later!

You can draw it this way, or any other way! It's up to you!

2. **Cut out the pig shape that you drew and lay it on top of the same piece of felt. Trace the shape so that you have two identical sides.** ⊕

3. **Now cut out the second pig shape, and you will have two sides of the pig.**

4. Pick one side of the pig. We're going to sew the face ☻ on! Do this by cutting out eyes with the black felt. You can add eyebrows too! Sew them on, then add the nostrils in any way you want!

5. Break out your needle and thread and sew the two pieces together. **Don't sew them completely shut, leave a little hole at the bottom to shove in the stuffing!**

6. **When you're done, add stuffing and then sew the opening up.**

7. Draw a tail in the pink felt. Cut it out and sew it onto the back.

Congrats! All done!

Pig Tip:
If you don't know how to sew, you can hot glue the two pieces together! 🐷

7

Image 16.4 Teagan Smyth
Teagan Smyth @TeagsWorld

Images 16.5-16.6 Teagan Smyth
Teagan Smyth @TeagsWorld

Images 16.7-16.8 Teagan Smyth
Teagan Smyth @TeagsWorld

FINISH THIS COMIC!

jarrettlerner.com

JARRETT!!

Image 16.9 Jarrett Lerner—finish this comic
Courtesy of Jarrett Lerner https://jarrettlerner.com/

school resources on his website, https://jarrettlerner.com/. You can also find links to his creative workbooks for students that we use in my own house!

Whatever introduction you choose to do, it is worth the time and effort to get students excited about being creators because the uses and reasons for making a comic are endless. Perhaps you can have students tell the story of a literary figure in a different setting (Images 16.10–16.12 MacPherson), or you can have your class practice second language conversations using visual clues, explain a concept, solve a global or local issue, etc. My daughter, Charlotte, wrote about the *Imaginary Voyages of Edgar Allan Poe* (created and written by Dwight L. MacPherson, Illustrated by Luis Czerniawski, Colored by Andrea Messi, Lettered by Simon Robins, and Edited by Rebecca MacPherson, Cover Illustration by Juan Ferreyra) after she excitedly read these comics in 7th grade. In her words:

> The Imaginary Voyage of Edgar Allan Poe is a comic book series all about the slightly insane writer, Mr. Poe. We all have read at least one of his short stories, like the *Black Cat*, *Telltale Heart*, and the *Gold Bug*. We also might have found ourselves wondering what exactly goes on in his head. Dwight MacPherson and team have taken what they know about Poe and created a graphic world of Poe's imagination. From talking rats to pale ghosts, this story weaves a believable path through the twists and turns of Poe's world. I personally have loved what was done with the Greek gods, namely Poseidon, the ruler of the ocean, in this story! I like to immerse myself in the original mythology, and I know about Thetis and the ocean nereids. Or maybe you recognize Charon, the ferryman of the River Styx. The amount of research put into this book is amazing, and you can feel the love Dwight MacPherson has for Poe. Not to mention the beautiful artwork by Luis Czerniawaski and Andrea Messi for the series! You can just tell what Poe is feeling from one glance at his expression, the blue of Virginia's ghost, and the deep caverns of Poseidon's palace. This is simply a must read, appealing especially to Poe lovers. My mom is an English teacher, and she is also a fan of Poe. She agrees that this is perfect for her classroom.

One lesson that worked really well for my students and me happened in our Pop Culture Club—a group that meets after school to discuss music, movies, TV, comics, prose books, etc. We wanted to make a comic but were unsure what topic to choose. We talked about the name of our town, Ambler, and the origins of this name. There were some rumors of a woman and a train crash. Not being from the area, my curiosity was piqued, especially since I had been teaching in the community for about 15 years at this point and had never thought about the name of the town. Being a history teacher, we immediately began to research and to ask people in the community, including parents, about the name of the town. We went to the local library and got in touch with the local historical society. The history was amazing, and yes, it did involve the efforts of a heroic woman after a disastrous head-on collision

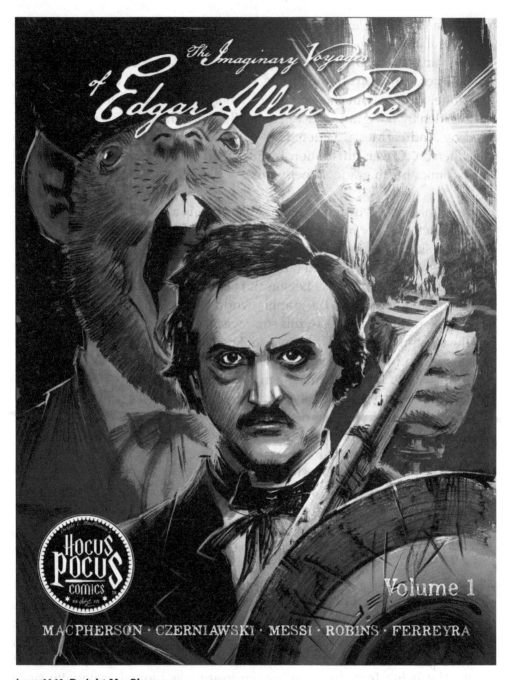

Image 16.10 Dwight MacPherson
(Interior pages):
Created and written by Dwight L. MacPherson
Hocus Pocus Comics https://www.hpcomics.net/
Illustrated by Luis Czerniawski
Colored by Andrea Messi
Lettered by Simon Robins
Edited by Rebecca MacPherson
(Cover): Cover Illustration by Juan Ferreyra

Image 16.11 **Dwight MacPherson**
(Interior pages):
Created and written by Dwight L. MacPherson
Hocus Pocus Comics https://www.hpcomics.net/
Illustrated by Luis Czerniawski
Colored by Andrea Messi
Lettered by Simon Robins
Edited by Rebecca MacPherson
(Cover): Cover Illustration by Juan Ferreyra

Image 16.12 Dwight MacPherson
(Interior pages):
Created and written by Dwight L. MacPherson
Hocus Pocus Comics https://www.hpcomics.net/
Illustrated by Luis Czerniawski
Colored by Andrea Messi
Lettered by Simon Robins
Edited by Rebecca MacPherson
(Cover): Cover Illustration by Juan Ferreyra

between two trains! Long story short, she charged onto the scene to help with the victims, and a legend was born. The students could not wait to make a comic about this real-life hero for whom their community was named!

Everyone wanted to be involved, but not all were sure how to go about it. We brainstormed different roles and got to work. We had students interviewing local historians, reading books, storyboarding, penciling, inking, and more. Some students, knowing how I create teacher guides for comics publishers, wanted to make their own lesson plans for teachers who might want to use this comic in their classrooms as well. This was an empowering experience for all involved, and we began brainstorming other people to research and create comics about. This could easily be adapted to your community or to any unit. Our next step is that I want to have my high school students share these comics with the elementary school students and really build community.

Clearly, comics are excellent for creating awareness and sharing personal stories. In my experience teaching with comics through the US State Department, I was lucky enough to meet the inspiring family behind the Bionic Kid comic (https://thebionickid.com/). In 2015, Zachary was the recipient of a prototype bionic arm from Limbitless Solutions when an idea began to form about creating a comic to empower others with this same experience. With now two comics published and sharing their story with the world, students in a similar situation can feel empowered. Using texts like this can model memoir making and individual story-telling. Students should be encouraged to tell their own stories and to create their own comics; this activity could easily be worked into a Language Arts class, an elementary class, or an advisory. It would energize individuals and foster relationships within the class and school (Images 16.13–16.16 BionicKid).

Image 16.13 Bionic Kid Issue #2
by Zachary Pamboukas (Author), Christo Pamboukas (Author), Niko Pamboukas (Author), Victor Davila (Illustrator), Matt Dombrowski (Editor) Limbitless Solutions, June 30, 2021

Image 16.14 Bionic Kid Issue #2
by Zachary Pamboukas (Author), Christo Pamboukas (Author), Niko Pamboukas (Author), Victor Davila (Illustrator), Matt Dombrowski (Editor)⎸Limbitless Solutions, June 30, 2021

Image 16.15 Bionic Kid Issue #2
by Zachary Pamboukas (Author), Christo Pamboukas (Author), Niko Pamboukas (Author), Victor Davila (Illustrator), Matt Dombrowski (Editor) Limbitless Solutions, June 30, 2021

Images 16.16 Bionic Kid Issue #2
by Zachary Pamboukas (Author), Christo Pamboukas (Author), Niko Pamboukas (Author), Victor Davila (Illustrator), Matt Dombrowski (Editor) Limbitless Solutions, June 30, 2021

Image 16.17 **Superman Red Son**
by Mark Millar (Author), Dave Johnson (Illustrator), Kilian Plunkett (Illustrator)
DC Comics February 1, 2004

There are many other powerful stories where the author overcomes certain limitations and chooses to tell their own story in order to inspire others. An author who has autism, Dave Kot, created his own comic books, *Face Value Comics*, to showcase how comics and social stories can greatly help those like him. There is a lot of research into comics and autism; much of this can be found on my website (TeachingWithComics.Com). Characters with autism can also be found in more popular titles, such as in Batman #80—Page Giant 2011, which has self-contained one-shot stories, including one from Joe Caramagna, Joe Lalich, Jack Purcell, and Wil Quintana, *One Lock, Many Keys*. In this story, there is a fight between Batman and Solomon Grundy, and a young boy turns his autism into a superpower to help Batman! In Chapter 17, you will read more about graphic memoirs and can use these books to inspire students to tell their own personal stories as well.

Comics often explore the concept of "what if" in society and can challenge our agreed-upon canon. DC has published multiple stories in their Elseworlds series, such as *Superman: Red Son*, Mark Millar, Dave Johnson, Kilian Plunkett, DC Comics Feb 2004. Kal El crash lands, not in Kansas, but in the Stalin controlled U.S.S.R. As Superman becomes a propaganda piece and hero for the Soviets, a deep question arises. Can Superman truly be a communist as no one can ever be his equal? There are many other stories in this series, and each one forces contemplation. Batman in the French Revolution, Batman hunting Jack the Ripper, the Flash taking the bullet meant for John F. Kennedy, and so many more. By having the reimagined fictional comics world collide with actual historical events, we can encourage students to do the same. Often, asking "what if" really forces our students to more fully showcase their understanding of the material (Images 16.17 Superman and 16.18 Batman).

Ultimately, comic making is an engaging and valuable tool for teaching students to explore and communicate their ideas in a focused and deliberate way. It builds community through cooperation and story-telling. It's flexible and can be adapted to a variety of topics, time constraints, and skills. And honestly, we can never underestimate the power of imagination and having fun while learning at all levels.

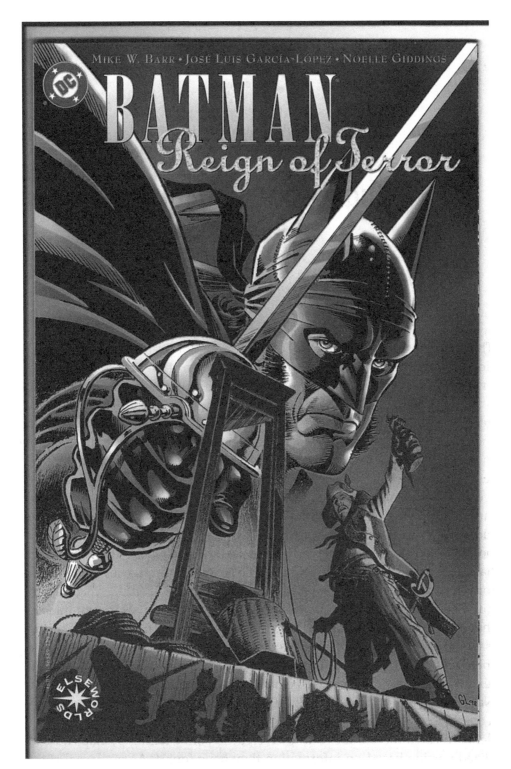

Image 16.18 Batman French Revolution
Jose Luis Garcia-Lopez cover artist, by Mike W Barr (Author)
DC Comics (January 1, 1999)

17

Refugees and Immigration

The global issue of displaced peoples, refugees, and obstacles to immigration is a topic of ever-growing importance. When students see news footage or read articles, they quickly become overwhelmed with the sheer number of affected people. Our minds deal with large volumes of information by generalizing and ignoring the individual. With comics, we can experience the plight of individuals and become emotionally and personally involved in their stories. In this lesson, I have several copies of multiple titles—each telling the story of a different person or group, and from different areas of the world. In this way, when we share out in small groups and then out to the large group, we can get a wide view of the issue while also seeing the individual. We can compare the different stories and see the common issues and potential solutions. As this topic occurs near the end of the year, I really don't have to hand out any specific worksheets as the students know what to look for when reading. I do ask that they keep a bulleted list of the major events, impactful panels to share, and their questions. When finished with the book, they do a small research project as they look into the historical and current issues surrounding where their story took place so that they can better help their group members to more fully understand the story in its wider context. When we are finished, we begin to do some research through the United Nations and brainstorm possible solutions. While I don't have students make a comic about this particular topic, it would be an engaging way to have students research these issues and then create a comic telling perhaps a fictionalized version based on information they have found. As my social studies

DOI: 10.4324/9781003291671-17

class focuses on making connections across time and peoples, my students always will make the connection to the Jewish Holocaust and the dangers of thinking of groups of people as "other".

For the historic fiction aspect of this project, my students and I discuss the comics history of heroes as immigrants and their acceptance into our societies—think Superman and Wonder Woman as an example. I have students read Laurie Halse Anderson's *Wonder Woman; Tempest Tossed,* illustrated by Leila del Duca, published by DC Comics, 2020 (Images 17.1–17.3). In this book, we see Wonder Woman as not only the immigrant she is, but also as a young woman trying to make sense of our world. As we read through this powerful story, we come across some rather heavy topics: trying to find yourself/adolescence, poverty, female empowerment, political prisoners, resistance to totalitarianism, child sex trafficking, child hunger, domestic violence, and the importance of the individual in making change. I was excited to have my own children read this engrossing story as it easily opened discussions about the current plight of peoples from around the world and why we need to pay attention. I could not have done this through other mediums. My own children, and my students, are then prepared to discuss and conduct more research to find ways to help.

Going from a fictional story based on real events, we then move on to other sources, such as the all-too-real autobiographical *When Stars Are Scattered*, by Victoria Jamieson and Omar Mohamed, Penguin Random House, 2020. This book, while marketed for younger readers, makes a difficult and vital topic accessible to all ages. (This is a rant for another time, but as a Reading Specialist, I tend to not limit students according to "reading level" or Lexile—just let them read!) We live the experiences of the author and his brother as they endure a life in a refugee camp in Kenya. While ultimately uplifting and inspiring, we see the love between brothers and community as they have to overcome many overwhelming obstacles in order to find a better life. This topic is one I am very passionate about and therefore have read and shared much on the topic with my students. By now, I am sure you can gather that I don't think we can underestimate the value of talking about the realities in the world, obstacles, and resiliency with our students. The illustrations in this book struck me in a powerful and human way because it was a true story in comic form, and it made me really see the plight of the refugee (Image 17.4 Stars).

Again, if this is a topic in your studies or discussions, then there are many immigration titles sharing a variety of experiences, much too many to share here. Many are full of despair and struggle; others are inspiring and uplifting. One unique approach to telling an immigrant story occurs in *Pie in the*

Image 17.1 Wonder Woman: Tempest Tossed
Laurie Halse Anderson author, Leila del Duca art
DC Comics; Illustrated edition (June 2, 2020)

Image 17.2 Wonder Woman: Tempest Tossed
Laurie Halse Anderson author, Leila del Duca art
DC Comics; Illustrated edition (June 2, 2020)

Image 17.3 Wonder Woman: Tempest Tossed
Laurie Halse Anderson author, Leila del Duca art
DC Comics; Illustrated edition (June 2, 2020)

Image 17.4 **When Stars Are Scattered**
by Victoria Jamieson, Omar Mohamed
Courtesy of Penguin Random House LLC

Image 17.5 Pie in the Sky
by Remy Lai (Author, Illustrator)
Henry Holt and Co. BYR Paperbacks; Illustrated edition (May 14, 2019)

Image 17.6 Pie in the Sky
by Remy Lai (Author, Illustrator)
Henry Holt and Co. BYR Paperbacks; Illustrated edition (May 14, 2019)

Image 17.7 Pie in the Sky
by Remy Lai (Author, Illustrator)
Henry Holt and Co. BYR Paperbacks; Illustrated edition (May 14, 2019)

Sky, by Remy Lai, Henry Holt, 2019. The book is formatted with prose and illustrations supporting each other, thus adding much depth and meaning to the story. One particular part of the book really struck me as an example of the power of comics as literature: We can talk to students about the alienation of moving into a new country, we can have them read prose on it, but in this story, the language barrier is depicted through nonsense symbols and conveyed through the confusion and fear shown on the kids' faces. In just a few images, the comic gets across a much deeper meaning of what it is like to be an outsider and the importance of being welcoming to others. It also demonstrates how well comics convey meaning despite language barriers (Images 17.5–17.7).

Because of the diverse nature of modern comics, immigrant stories can be found within a wide range of superhero stories as well. One of my favorite heroes, Ms. Marvel, or Kamala Khan, is a Pakistani-American teen from Jersey City and is part of my favorite hero team, the Champions. Co-creator and author G. Willow Wilson has a wonderful TedxRainier about her initial thoughts when approached to write this new hero, titled *A Superhero for Generation Why*, 2016. Initially, she was hesitant and feared receiving hate mail over the ethnicity of the character. However, as we know, Ms. Marvel is a highly successful comic title and will be a show on Disney+. In the comic, Kamala has to fight not only the typical villains, but also against prejudice and misunderstanding of her family. Turns out, she is just like everyone else, just a regular teenager trying to fit in.

It is this reality that we are all different, that we all come from different families and different experiences, but that we are all human with similar dreams and fears that needs to be at the heart of our discussions. When studying a topic such as immigration and refugees, it is important to remember that there isn't one version—one type of story or one experience. Comics are a wonderful way to bring a variety of perspectives, and it's often as simple as showing a picture of a girl in a hijab. When we read prose, the default of many readers is to imagine the main characters as white, but in comics, the perspective and characterization are immediate and impactful.

18

Social-Emotional Learning and Graphic Memoirs

Comics allow the reader to literally see themselves in the story and to become emotionally involved, even responsible for the characters. We have already discussed the wonderful representation seen in comics today in terms of race and identity. There is also a growing number of titles that directly address social-emotional learning as well. In education, we know that we need to see the whole student, not just test scores. We know that learning cannot happen until students feel safe and cared for. Sometimes, just having a diverse collection of books in the classroom and library can be enough to literally save the lives of students as they feel seen and accepted. We also need to consider the school counselor and mental health professional space, as well as the home library. Comics are enticing and welcoming to read, and students will often gravitate to them first. There are many titles that can open up vital conversations in ways that might not otherwise be possible. I can speak to my own experiences as a parent based on discussions I've had with my own children through comics.

A few years ago, my youngest daughter had to have dental surgery and multiple teeth pulled from the front of her mouth. She was absolutely terrified of going to school and being made fun of by other students. She thought that she was the only one who had undergone this type of procedure and just couldn't fathom going to school. However, I gave her a copy of the graphic memoir *Smile*, by Raina Telgemeier. My daughter literally saw herself in the images in the comic and immediately began to feel seen. Knowing that this was a true story also helped to further calm her nerves and not feel so alone.

DOI: 10.4324/9781003291671-18

When she went to school, she was able to reference the graphic novel and inspired other students to read it as well. And *Smile* is not the only graphic memoir that has directly helped situations within my own family. We have read books about body image, eating disorders, anxiety, and more. As a father, one particular book really helped me talk to my daughter about getting her period for the first time. We read *Go With the Flow* by Lily Williams and Karen Schneemann together and discussed not only changes in life, but also female empowerment and speaking up. I can just imagine the power of having resources like these available in the school counselor office. A pamphlet or prose text simply does not engage a reader in the same way as these graphic novels.

These types of comics not only help individuals to feel seen, but also allow the reader to see the experiences of other people from different backgrounds. This is the absolute power of having diverse reading clubs in schools. I am proud to be an advisor of one in my High School and a participant along with my own children in their school. This nationwide club is called Project Lit and was started by an inspiring teacher, Jarred Amato, who saw a need to share culturally relevant and current literature with his students. The students choose what books they want to read and discuss from an ever-growing list of Young Adult and Middle Grade books nominated by each individual club. The foremost purpose of this club is to have students read stories that are relevant and open vital conversations about the world around them. In this club, we certainly read prose books about race and identity—such as *Ghost Boys* by Jewell Parker Rhodes, *The Hate You Give* by Angie Thomas, *They Both Die at the End* by Adam Silvera, and so many other powerful titles. As part of these selections, we also read and discuss graphic memoirs as part of this experience.

One such memoir that we read is *New Kid*, by Jerry Craft, which has the proud distinction of being the first graphic novel to win the Newbery Medal! This novel is semi-autobiographical based on the experiences of Jerry and his sons. We were lucky enough to not only have Jerry Skype in with my high school students, but also to have him as part of my own kids' Project Lit meeting in their middle school. Importantly, this book opens conversations about race and judgement, but in an accessible and human way. Jerry uses the full power of graphic novels to get across depth and meaning that would not be possible in prose. My son felt connected to the main character, Jordan, even though they both have had different life experiences. However, he was able to connect through Jordan's love of pop culture and comics. I was also lucky enough to meet Jerry at New York Comic Con, and he gave me an autographed advanced reader's copy of New Kid for my son to read. In a house full of books, this is my son's most prized possession and is prominently displayed in his bedroom library. Liam was moved when he read this book and wanted to share his love for it with other readers his age. Liam wrote a review of the book, and he had me share it on social media. My three kids now often read and review many books and share on #SmythReads. My son's review when he was in 5th grade:

I love Jerry Craft's new book, New Kid! I love that we keep seeing Jordan's drawings in his notebook—it really helped me get to know him. He's a lot like me because he likes superheroes and wants superpowers—he wants to be like Batman who has a jet, so he doesn't need to fly like Superman. Batman is more human than Superman. In one part, Jordan wrote about how he wanted to be Batman and not just because he's rich, but because he can fit in anywhere and stands up for the little guys. I was also a new kid in a new school and I felt some of the same feelings Jordan did. We can't judge people so much and I didn't like how some of the kids could be mean, but I thought Jordan was brave like superheroes and found a good superhero team of friends. I think kids (and adults!) could learn a lot from this book on how to treat one another. This book is great for a classroom! When he is in different places, Jordan has to act differently and I don't know why we can't just be ourselves. He loves to play video games too, just like me. It doesn't matter what color we are or how much money we have—be human!

Another graphic memoir we read was *Hey, Kiddo* by Jarrett Krosoczka, which gave us powerful insight into the life of a child being raised by his grandparents because his mother was addicted to drugs and his father was not a part of this life. As I read this book with my students, it really served as an important reminder that everyone is going through something in life and that we can't lose sight of this when focusing on the day-to-day goings-on in school. Books like this remind us that we need to see the whole student and to be understanding of what life might be throwing their way. This memoir, though absolutely devastating, was also full of humor, hope, and love. I know that I have students in similar situations, and this book can be a source of comfort and power for them. However, it is also important that their classmates who are unfamiliar with these situations also realize that not everything is as it may seem and that kindness and grace should be shared with everyone.

Also this year, we read George Takei's graphic memoir, *They Called Us Enemy*, based on his experiences as a child in Japanese-American Internment

Camps. It was particularly timely as there has been an increasing growth of racism against Asian-Americans, which led to our students requesting that we read this book. While I have taught about these camps in my history course, we had not yet had the chance to look at *They Called Us Enemy*. After reading this book with my Project Lit Club, I am excited to share it with my students in the upcoming school years. It launched us into a really in-depth discussion about how Americans sometimes treat each other, especially as the "other". When we discuss historical events, it can be hard for students to connect to so many important factors going on at the same time. Graphic memoirs, like *They Called Us Enemy*, allow us to slow down a bit and really humanize the history. As we discussed the book, students immediately made connections to the AAPI racism being experienced today, but also to the Civil Rights Movement of the 1960s. We talked about how this movement was not just a "black and white" issue, that it is still ongoing, and that we need to understand the history to enact change today. We were absolutely lucky enough to have the co-authors and brilliant artist of the book Zoom in with our students and larger school community. As part of our discussion, I also shared how comics were used during WWII to perpetuate racial stereotypes of Asian peoples, especially between Japanese and Chinese ethnicities. (Images 18.1–18.3).

For LBGTQIA+ discussions, there is a wonderful, growing amount of titles that are geared for readers of all ages. Not only will comics like these help students with internal questions of who they are, but they also, as always with comics, help us see one another for who we are. When I was a student, I had no real experience with literature of non-straight characters and really did not have a window into this world until I was older. This is not something that should happen, and I am thrilled that my own children are growing up in a wonderfully diverse world of heroes. We see an increasing number of lesbian, gay, fluid, and transgender characters in comics and graphic novels. These titles open up communication and perspective and allow students to explore their feelings. Often, it is just having these books in my classroom that makes students feel welcome, safe, and seen. There are too many wonderful titles to list, and again, I'll refer you to TeachingWithComics.com for lists of titles organized by topic.

I have even presented at comic book conventions on panels discussing using comics as therapy and how they lead to powerful conversations between us, the panelists, and the audience. There are wonderful titles that can help us in so many ways as we cope with the struggles of life. Again, my website, TeachingWithComics.com, has lists of comics that I recommend, and I continually update it. I have used these books with my own children, including books on eating disorders and identification. There is a comic about losing a loved one to ALS, and this helped me with my own grief over losing

Image 18.1 They Called Us Enemy
They Called Us Enemy © George Takei, courtesy Top Shelf Productions/IDW Publishing

Image 18.2 They Called Us Enemy
They Called Us Enemy © George Takei, courtesy Top Shelf Productions/IDW Publishing

126

Image 18.3 They Called Us Enemy
They Called Us Enemy © George Takei, courtesy Top Shelf Productions/IDW Publishing

Image 18.4 Green Lanterns
Green Lanterns #15: Ghosts of the Past. DC Comics Jan 18, 2017. Sam Humphries author, Miguel Mendonca pencils, Scott Hanna inks, Tomeu Morey and Tyler Kirkham cover.

my own father to this disease as I saw myself in the pages. Jane Foster, as the Mighty Thor, has suffered through breast cancer, and many have written in how this has helped them keep fighting through their own struggle against cancer.

In particular, there is one image that I have hanging near my desk at home and school as it reminds me to keep making the heroic choice. I have social anxiety and depression, and it can often be difficult to just get out of bed in the morning, to enter the world. In this image, we see Jessica Cruz, of the Green Lanterns, also fighting through her anxiety on a wonderfully illustrated page. I share this image with my students in the beginning of the year as I openly discuss that we are all going through something, and we need to see the human in front of us. As a Green Lantern, whose strength comes from will power, this is a powerful battle for her and resonates with my students and me (Image 18.4 Green Lanterns).

19

Think Outside the Comic

By this point in the book, I am hoping your mind is swirling with many practical ways that comics can assist you in creating a community of readers in your school. In this chapter, I hope to generate a few more ideas with you, and most of them can be tailored for elementary or secondary, or better yet, be a true community event for all ages. If you're feeling particularly inspired and energetic, consider creating a pop culture or comic book club at your school or in your library. In my school, this is an after-school activity where students gather to read comics, discuss superheroes, make comics, watch movies, whatever those students enjoy in any given year. I have seen such wonderful learning and inclusiveness happen in these clubs at my own school. Also, look within the confines of your existing school day. You might be able to make time during the school day in study hall or other rest periods; I happily offer a read comics and chill session during an activity period that's included in my school schedule—students just come in, borrow a book or bring their own, and read comics. I often have students from our autistic support program come in and share their knowledge of comics, and we draw together. I really have found, both in school and in public, that the comics community is so welcoming and inclusive.

One AMAZING idea is to create a comic book convention for your school or library! I have helped organize many and have also been invited as a guest speaker as well. This is such a great way to get students from across the district/area to get involved in the planning and carrying out of the convention. Some ideas for a fun and valuable convention include these suggestions:

DOI: 10.4324/9781003291671-19

Don't do it all yourself—reach out to school clubs and local organizations. Make students an integral part of the event. Each student group can be responsible for sponsoring a different activity. Get other teachers and staff members involved. Reach out to your district's social media people and the community.

Don't be shy about reaching out to your favorite creators to come and present—either in person or virtually. Be honest about your budget when reaching out—some will have presentation fees where others will not. Consider zoom options if travel constraints are an issue.

Be organized—just like in a "normal" convention, there is the floor and then panel rooms. We carry out the organization of the school convention in the same way. A large room, such as the gym or lunchroom, is used to have an area of tables. Invite local artists, authors, organizations, etc., to come in and sell their products. The school can charge a fee for each table that they rent.

Create Panels—these usually run 45 to 90 minutes and can be on many topics. You might have some featured guests who will talk about their comics process, etc. Students can run trivia sessions on pop culture with comics as prizes. You can also run an educator track with panels focused on the use of comics in the classroom.

Photo and selfie stations—always a big hit! Ask students to create wood cutouts and paint them as superheroes or other pop culture icons. Leave a hole for the participant's face and take pictures. Paint or buy a city landscape on a wall as a great superhero backdrop. Provide picture props. Create a hashtag for students to post their pictures.

Cosplay Competitions—students love to dress up. Have different categories—perhaps separated by age and/or genre.

Craft stations—make lightsabers from pool noodles and electrical tape, superhero puppets from brown paper bags, accessory making (tiara for Wonder Woman, necklace for Black Panther, etc.), etc. This is where your student organizations (student government, Kiwanis, Sports teams, drama club, etc.) can get involved. Each can choose, organize, gather materials, and manage a different table for a craft. They can help the children who visit to finish their crafts as well. This is great for teaching service as well as building school community.

Comic contest—have different age categories and have students submit their own original comics ahead of time. With a group of judges, award prizes on the day of the convention. Display the winners/entrants on a placard.

A comic book convention can also be held on a smaller scale or could be more focused on literacy and skill-building. With this focus in mind, I have helped multiple school districts create early literacy nights in their elementary schools. As an educator and Reading Specialist, I fully understand the vital importance of early literacy. We've created fun nights where students and their parents go through different stations, often in the cafeteria, and complete different literacy activities, culminating in a bag of books, games, and literacy activities to bring home. We have stations where students read to others, where parent and teacher volunteers read to students, where students write short stories, and where they use my sequencing activity from Chapter 7—where we provide blank comic book templates, and we encourage students to see reading as exciting. While the focus is mostly on literacy, it can have a superhero flare. You can invite students and adults to dress up. You can include craft stations, invite local authors, and make it a fun family and educational event.

At any of these events, getting books into the hands of our students, especially the younger ones, is so important. Not every child has a home library, and some do not own books of their own. I love when these young students look absolutely thrilled when they realize that these books now belong to them after our activities. We can not only make this happen through literacy nights and comic book conventions, but also through more deliberate outreach. Enlist local businesses and ask them to host a book box of donated books that children can read and take when they visit. Our school has done this, and teacher volunteers visit the boxes to refill them from time to time. Expand on this idea and have the barber ask young customers to read to them when getting a haircut. This is a wonderful, mutually beneficial way to create a community involved in the education of our students. Get student organizations involved or as older students to help you keep the boxes stocked. Ask community members to donate books. Little libraries can also be put out into parks playgrounds when building a small container full of books; in our school, students must complete a senior project, and several of the students chose to create little libraries. Of course, these can be made through the local tech school or by a capable woodworker. However, we also reached out to the local paper company and asked if they had any old newspaper bins—remember the ones where you put in coins and pulled out the paper? Turns out, they had a warehouse full of them, and they were more than happy to donate them to us; they even removed the coin-operated lock. We then had the students decorate them by painting colorful literary characters and placed these bins out into the community! Don't forget to join forces with other existing programs. Little libraries were placed outside of Little

League, and free, high-interest books were given out through a community program offering free bagged meals at the township building. Not only were children able to pick up food, but we also put out free book bins, talked about titles, and encouraged families to take what they want. When getting these books into the hands of readers, be mindful in the representation you offer in the choices. Of course, I always include comics and graphic novels and can't tell you how excited kids are to take them home! Funnily enough, I also have adults sheepishly ask me if they can take a comic, and I am more than happy to say yes and to talk comics with them!

Beyond that, I look at comic book conventions as professional development for myself as well. Whether I am attending a school comic convention or a national one, it is always a chance to hear from creators, about history, about the publication process, etc. It is a chance for me to ask questions, to be re-energized, to share ideas, to hear new ideas, to meet other professionals, to have fun, to be inspired.

It gives me a chance to remember that there is value in what we do and what we offer and to look at the world from other perspectives. Many educators, like myself, attend traditional education conferences to hear authors talk and to attend panel discussions on important educational topics. Comic book conventions, especially larger ones, are often run the same, with differences of course! You can spend days sitting in on panels with experts discussing pop culture and its impact on the world. I have sat in on panels given by the Smithsonian on using comics as literature and the Library of Congress showcasing their amazing comics collection, to name a few.

20

Final Thoughts

I cannot thank you enough for buying this book, and also for taking a chance on learning more about teaching with comics. I hope this book gave you some ideas that you can use in your classroom tomorrow, but more than that, I want these ideas to marinate and to spark your own lesson ideas. My advice is to just start somewhere. Choose a comic from this book or just pick one up from the library. When you go to the local bookstore, check out the comic section. Find your local comic book shop, ask the clerk for suggestions, and browse the racks. I read comics all the time with the idea that maybe the books have something that can be used with my students. Sometimes it's just one panel, sometimes an entire book, but the stories all help to energize me and to keep me learning. Additionally, I find it valuable to get involved in the vast community of people who read, discuss, and create comics. While I may not love every comic I read, they all help to widen my perspective and to broaden my experience because that's what books and comics do. They bring humanity closer. Comics are truly global.

I also love that social media means that this chapter won't be the last word as we now share this comics-in-education journey together. My website, TeachingWithComics.com, is continually updated with ideas and lessons, book referrals, and so much more. It would be impossible to include everything in one book, just like it's impossible to share everything during a presentation. However, I can be reached on Twitter and Instagram on @HistoryComics. You can join the wonderfully collaborative Facebook group, Comic Book Teachers. You can follow and share ideas on my personal

DOI: 10.4324/9781003291671-20

Facebook page, Teaching With Comics. I may wind up meeting you in person at a comic book convention or education conference. Your district or organization may bring me out to present to you and your colleagues. I hope to see you soon, either virtually or in person.

Final thoughts—if you are not sharing the awesomeness of your classroom, think about it. Blog about it. Share on social media. Present at a convention. We need you.

Appendix: Complete Teacher Guides

Image 4.2 American Born Chinese
From AMERICAN BORN CHINESE by Gene Luen Yang. Copyright © 2006 by Gene Luen Yang. Reprinted by permission of First Second, an imprint of Roaring Brook Press, a division of Holtzbrinck Publishing Holdings Limited Partnership. All Rights Reserved.

Discussion Questions:

1. What does it mean to be "All-American"?
2. After reading the book, go back and discuss how the story of the Monkey King paralleled that of Jin Wang. (For example, on p. 20, the Monkey King now recognizes his own smell. Why? Later, compare this to Jin's transformation into and out of Danny on p. 214.)
3. Why do you think so many people want to immigrate to the United States? How does this tie into the idea of the American Dream? Why is FOB an insult?
4. Ethnic stereotypes play a large role in this book—discuss their impact on both the characters and you as a reader.
5. Pp. 55–85 Tze-Yo-Tzuh—what is his message to the Monkey King? What is the message to the reader?

Brief Teaching Recommendations for Educators and Readers

1. As you read through the book, keep a journal detailing the parallels between the Monkey King and Jin Wang's lives.
2. P. 102—idioms. Define the term and come up with as many examples as possible. Choose one to draw in a literal interpretation. See if a classmate can guess the idiom.
3. Pp. 133–160 Morality story. What is the moral of this story? Create your own morality story in a short comic.
4. This story is a memoir; therefore, identity of self is a large part of this story. Write a short memoir about a time in your life when you felt like an outsider or questioned who you are/want to be. Make an illustration of this moment to summarize your feelings.
5. Rewrite one of the moments in the book that you wish you could change. How would this change alter the message in the story?

Suggested Common Core Standards Alignment—Because they encompass the ultimate goal for reading literature in grades 9 through 12, the most relevant Common Core Standards for 11th- and 12th-grade literature are listed here.

CCSS.ELA-LITERACY.RL.11–12.1 Cite strong and thorough textual evidence to support analysis of what the text says explicitly as well as inferences drawn from the text, including determining where the text leaves matters uncertain.

CCSS.ELA-LITERACY.RL.11–12.1 Cite strong and thorough textual evidence to support analysis of what the text says explicitly as well as inferences drawn from the text, including determining where the text leaves matters uncertain.

CCSS.ELA-LITERACY.RL.11–12.3 Analyze the impact of the author's choices regarding how to develop and relate elements of a story or drama (e.g., where a story is set, how the action is ordered, how the characters are introduced and developed).

CCSS.ELA-LITERACY.RL.11–12.4 Determine the meaning of words and phrases as they are used in the text, including figurative and connotative meanings; analyze the impact of specific word choices on meaning and tone, including words with multiple meanings or language that is particularly fresh, engaging, or beautiful

CCSS.ELA-LITERACY.RL.11–12.5 Analyze how an author's choices concerning how to structure specific parts of a text (e.g., the choice of where to begin or end a story, the choice to provide a comedic or tragic resolution) contribute to its overall structure and meaning as well as its aesthetic impact.

CCSS.ELA-LITERACY.RL.11–12.6 Analyze a case in which grasping a point of view requires distinguishing what is directly stated in a text from what is really meant (e.g., satire, sarcasm, irony, or understatement).

A Wrinkle In Time
Madeleine L'Engle
Adapted by Hope Larson
Square Fish, 2015

Discussion Questions

1. Ever have a day/week like Meg does in the beginning of the story? How do you cope?
2. Visual Evidence—throughout the story, some panels are shaded differently than others. What meaning do you think the artist, Hope Larson, was trying to illustrate through this contrast?
3. Why did Meg and Charles Wallace pretend to be dumb? Why do we sometimes put on a false facade to fit in?
4. Mrs. Who gives quotes throughout the book—which is your favorite? Why? How do these quotes support the themes expressed at those moments in the story?
5. P. 140 describes a fifth dimension and time travel—do you think this theory or similar ones are possible?
6. What do you think about IT's perfect world? Would you want to live in that type of world? Why or why not? Why do you think some people would want this type of governance? Is equality being exactly the same? What should equality look like?

Brief Teaching Recommendations for Educators and Readers (Note—this book presents exciting opportunities to have cross-curricular lessons between Language Arts, social studies, and Science.)

1. Conduct a text-to-text comparison between a scene in the prose book and one in the graphic novel. What are the advantages and limitations of each format? (Two possible examples from the graphic novel can be found on pp. 121–134, when Mrs. Whatsit transforms, or p. 104 when they tesseract.)
2. On pp. 157–158, several well-known historical persons are discussed as being fighters for earth against IT. What other individual from history would you choose to fight against the darkness? Why? Draw your choice as a superhero. What would their powers be?
3. Pp. 356–357—In what ways is life like a sonnet? Write a sonnet about your life (real or imagined).

Suggested Common Core Standards Alignment—Because they encompass the ultimate goal for reading literature in grades 9 through 12, the most relevant Common Core Standards for 11th- and 12th-grade literature are listed here.

CCSS.ELA-LITERACY.RL.11–12.7 Analyze multiple interpretations of a story, drama, or poem (e.g., recorded or live production of a play or recorded novel or poetry), evaluating how each version interprets the source text. **(Compare the graphic novel to the prose version and/or the movie.)**

CCSS.ELA-LITERACY.RL.11–12.1 Cite strong and thorough textual evidence to support analysis of what the text says explicitly as well as inferences drawn from the text, including determining where the text leaves matters uncertain.

CCSS.ELA-LITERACY.RL.11–12.2 Determine two or more themes or central ideas of a text and analyze their development over the course of the text, including how they interact and build on one another to produce a complex account; provide an objective summary of the text.

CCSS.ELA-LITERACY.RL.11–12.3 Analyze the impact of the author's choices regarding how to develop and relate elements of a story or drama (e.g., where a story is set, how the action is ordered, how the characters are introduced and developed).

CCSS.ELA-LITERACY.RL.11–12.4 Determine the meaning of words and phrases as they are used in the text, including figurative and connotative meanings; analyze the impact of specific word choices on meaning and tone, including words with multiple meanings or language that is particularly fresh, engaging, or beautiful

CCSS.ELA-LITERACY.RL.11–12.5 Analyze how an author's choices concerning how to structure specific parts of a text (e.g., the choice of where to begin or end a story, the choice to provide a comedic or tragic resolution) contribute to its overall structure and meaning as well as its aesthetic impact.

CCSS.ELA-LITERACY.RL.11–12.6 Analyze a case in which grasping a point of view requires distinguishing what is directly stated in a text from what is really meant (e.g., satire, sarcasm, irony, or understatement).

Real Friends/Best Friends
Shannon Hale and LeUyen Pham
First Second, 2017 and 2019

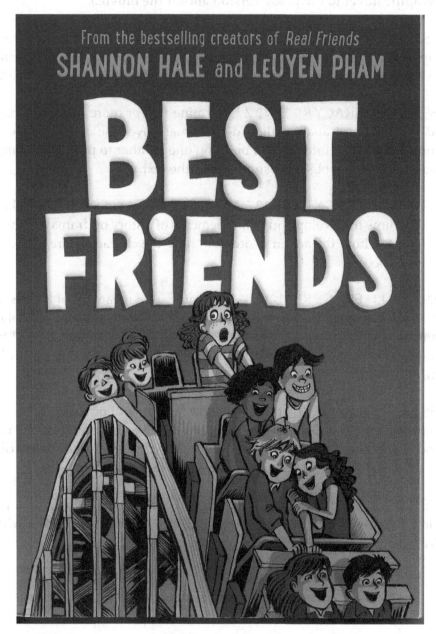

Image A.1 Best Friends
From BEST FRIENDS by Shannon Hale, illustrated by LeUyen Pham. Text copyright © 2019 by Shannon Hale. Illustrations copyright © 2019 by LeUyen Pham. Reprinted by permission of First Second, an imprint of Roaring Brook Press, a division of Holtzbrinck Publishing Holdings Limited Partnership. All Rights Reserved.

Image A.2 Real Friends

From REAL FRIENDS by Shannon Hale, illustrated by LeUyen Pham. Text copyright © 2017 by Shannon Hale. Illustrations copyright © 2017 by LeUyen Pham. Reprinted by permission of First Second, an imprint of Roaring Brook Press, a division of Holtzbrinck Publishing Holdings Limited Partnership. All Rights Reserved.

Discussion Questions

1. What is a memoir? What are the advantages to telling a personal story in graphic novel form?
2. Throughout the stories, there is a repetition of, "Everyone needs a friend." What is a real friend? A best friend? What characteristics are needed? How does having a friend cause Shannon to be different? Does she feel braver? More imaginative? Confident? Strong?
3. How is Shannon different when she does not feel like she has a friend? Compare this to how her older sister, Jenny, or Vance act when excluded. Explore the various ways people may react when not feeling like they fit in: with anxiety, with anger, by lying or hiding, with repetitive behaviors.
4. The Group. Discuss cliques/social hierarchy at school and home. Why do the girls follow along with Jen and the group rules? What is the danger in walking away?
5. What do Zara and Veronica teach Shannon about being cool and being a friend? Does their popularity come from exclusion? How does this change Shannon? Change the playground atmosphere? Change Jen? How does Shannon carry this influence into her next year of school?
6. What is the significance of Shannon choosing the classes that she wants instead of the classes the group chose together? Why is she hopeful rather than afraid? What has Shannon learned about friendship?
7. What is the significance of Shannon's imaginative world? Should real friends support and value this talent? How do her daydreams and stories parallel her experiences in real life?

Brief Teaching Recommendations for Educators and Readers

1. Write a short memoir of a time in your life about you and your friends. Turn it into a comic.
2. Is Shannon a good friend? If you were Shannon's friend, choose a place in the book to give her advice about dealing with the group or being a friend to others. Redraw the page(s) that you decided to change.
3. Sometimes, navigating social expectations is confusing to Shannon. She repeatedly references "the rules" and gets frustrated by them

constantly changing. Choose a rule that you have also struggled with or one that you have successfully navigated and write down a piece of advice for others. As a class, combine your rules as a guide to positive relationships.

4. Write your own guide to being a friend. What qualities do you think are needed in order to be a good friend to others? Include qualities you look for in others or that you feel you show to others.

This memoir explores friendship dynamics in the middle grades, so the most relevant core standards for that age group are listed here:

CCSS.ELA-LITERACY.RL.6.1 Cite textual evidence to support analysis of what the text says explicitly as well as inferences drawn from the text.

CCSS.ELA-LITERACY.RL.6.2 Determine a theme or central idea of a text and how it is conveyed through particular details; provide a summary of the text distinct from personal opinions or judgments.

CCSS.ELA-LITERACY.RL.6.3 Describe how a particular story's or drama's plot unfolds in a series of episodes as well as how the characters respond or change as the plot moves toward a resolution.

CCSS.ELA-LITERACY.RL.6.4 Determine the meaning of words and phrases as they are used in a text, including figurative and connotative meanings; analyze the impact of a specific word choice on meaning and tone

CCSS.ELA-LITERACY.RL.6.5 Analyze how a particular sentence, chapter, scene, or stanza fits into the overall structure of a text and contributes to the development of the theme, setting, or plot.

CCSS.ELA-LITERACY.RL.6.6 Explain how an author develops the point of view of the narrator or speaker in a text.

Speak
Laurie Halse Anderson and Emily Carroll
Farrar, Straus, and Giroux (BYR); 2nd edition (February 6, 2018)

FOR A MORE IN-DEPTH TEACHER GUIDE, SEE https://www.mackidss-choolandlibrary.com/teachers-guide-speak-the-graphic-novel/

Discussion Questions

1. Ask the students to create a list of the top ten lies people have told them about high school. Allow students to share their ideas with the class. Compare to those given in the graphic novel.
2. Choose a favorite part of the graphic novel and compare it to the prose book—examples: P. 103 in the graphic novel and the sculpture. . . . The rape by IT. . . . The janitor's closet. . . .
3. On page 275, how does Mr. Freeman's advice to Melinda about the tree convey the theme of the story? Can you connect this to other examples in the book?
4. From pp. 297–300, Melinda struggles with the question, "Was I raped?" What are the myths about rape that are revealed here? What is the significance of her internal conflict?
5. On pp. 347–363—how does this section revisit the images and symbols used throughout the book? How does Melinda regain her voice and her power?

Brief Teaching Recommendations for Educators and Readers

1. **A Call to Action**—Melinda finds herself unable to speak because she fears how others might view her following the rape. Sadly, the victims of sexual assault often feel powerless a second time in trying to deal with the aftermath of their attack. With the #MeToo movement, many are calling for more attention to the issue, more support for the victims, and more accountability for the assailants. Ask students to research the issue of sexual assault and the movement by reading credible print and digital sources. Students should then draft a speech proposing initiatives in schools, the community, or in the nation that are intended to educate people on sexual assault; or they can write a speech asking the school board, the town council, or the government to implement preventative measures, provide resources for victims, pass legislation, etc. Using the visual medium, students can also create awareness posters, videos, etc.
2. **Socratic Seminar**—the story begins with Melinda saying, "I am an outcast", which sets the tone of isolation in the story. Consider how the graphic novel depicts this isolation. Assign students the task of recording specific examples of this isolation throughout the graphic novel. (These examples can be both verbal and nonverbal, such as

Melinda being hunched over, facial expression, etc.) Create a Socratic Seminar class and tell students to come prepared with their textual and visual evidence. What is the impact of each of these pieces of evidence on Melinda, both positive and negative?

3. **Research Allusions**—throughout the story, there are references to famous fictional and real-life figures that are meant to parallel Melinda's experiences and emotions. Give students a list of these references: Dracula, Maya Angelou, Nathaniel Hawthorne and Hester Prynne, Ariel, Gregor Mendel, Pablo Picasso, and the Suffragettes. In pairs, or individually, have students research one of these references and present their findings to the class. How do the depictions of these figures connect to Melinda's journey?

4. **What Happens Next?** Speak ends with Melinda stating, "I'm not going to let it kill me, I can grow." Ask students to brainstorm the next chapter of the book—perhaps the very next day or years in the future. Have them create a comic of this chapter or illustrate one particular scene.

Suggested Common Core Standards Alignment—Because they encompass the ultimate goal for reading literature in grades 9 through 12, the most relevant Common Core Standards for 9th- and 10th-grade literature are listed here.

CCSS.ELA-LITERACY.RL.11–12.1 Cite strong and thorough textual evidence to support analysis of what the text says explicitly as well as inferences drawn from the text, including determining where the text leaves matters uncertain.

CCSS.ELA-LITERACY.RL.11–12.2 Determine two or more themes or central ideas of a text and analyze their development over the course of the text, including how they interact and build on one another to produce a complex account; provide an objective summary of the text.

CCSS.ELA-LITERACY.RL.11–12.3 Analyze the impact of the author's choices regarding how to develop and relate elements of a story or drama (e.g., where a story is set, how the action is ordered, how the characters are introduced and developed).

CCSS.ELA-LITERACY.RL.11–12.4 Determine the meaning of words and phrases as they are used in the text, including figurative and connotative meanings; analyze the impact of specific word choices on meaning and tone, including words with multiple meanings or language that is particularly fresh, engaging, or beautiful. (Include Shakespeare as well as other authors.)

CCSS.ELA-LITERACY.RL.11–12.5 Analyze how an author's choices concerning how to structure specific parts of a text (e.g., the choice of where to begin or end a story, the choice to provide a comedic or tragic resolution) contribute to its overall structure and meaning as well as its aesthetic impact.

CCSS.ELA-LITERACY.RL.11–12.6 Analyze a case in which grasping a point of view requires distinguishing what is directly stated in a text from what is really meant (e.g., satire, sarcasm, irony, or understatement).

CCSS.ELA-LITERACY.RL.11–12.7 Analyze multiple interpretations of a story, drama, or poem (e.g., recorded or live production of a play or recorded novel or poetry), evaluating how each version interprets the source text.

Olympians
George O'Connor
First Second; First Edition (January 5, 2010)

From OLYMPIANS: ZEUS: KING OF THE GODS by George O'Connor. Copyright © 2010 by George O'Connor. Reprinted by permission of First Second, an imprint of Roaring Brook Press, a division of Holtzbrinck Publishing Holdings Limited Partnership. All Rights Reserved.

Discussion Questions

1. Why do we assign human traits to the gods? What are those traits?
2. It's been said that modern superheroes are the new gods—they have taken the place of the Greek gods. Do you agree? What modern superheroes have their roots in Greek mythology?
3. What morals/lessons from these stories can still apply to today? Why do you think that Greek Mythology has such a large impact on our current world?
4. Which god would you want to be? Why?

Brief Teaching Recommendations for Educators and Readers

1. Create a new god for the world of today, complete with an origin story. What obstacle(s) would they have to overcome? Draw this new god. What powers would they have? Where would they live? What would their outfit look like? (Or even create yourself as this new god. What would your quest be?)
2. Research the story of the god depicted in one of the myths in this series. What would you have added to the comic you read? Draw this additional scene. Possible research sources—https://www. theoi.com/greek-mythology/greek-gods.html, https://www. greekmythology.com/ https://www.ducksters.com/history/ ancient_greek_mythology.php https://pantheon.org/mythology/ greek/
3. The myths convey lessons to the readers, but not all of the messages are necessarily positive. Explore the stories more deeply—pull evidence from the story and explain the lessons, cultural beliefs, or values that you feel are being taught or criticized through the story.
4. Create a Greek Mythology family tree as a class or as an individual. For each, include their name, a symbol, a succinct summary, and a picture of how you feel they should be depicted. This can be done in a video format or a traditional bulletin board form.
5. Research to see if there are similar gods in different cultures to the ones you read about in the Greek Mythology series. What do these parallels reveal about people and what we value or question in our world? Be sure to consider symbols, obstacles, and their explanations of natural phenomenons.

Suggested Common Core Standards Alignment—Because they encompass the ultimate goal for reading literature in grades 9 through 12, the most relevant Common Core Standards for 11th- and 12th-grade literature are listed here.

CCSS.ELA-LITERACY.RL.11–12.1 Cite strong and thorough textual evidence to support analysis of what the text says explicitly as well as inferences drawn from the text, including determining where the text leaves matters uncertain.

CCSS.ELA-LITERACY.RL.11–12.2 Determine two or more themes or central ideas of a text and analyze their development over the course of the text, including how they interact and build on one another to produce a complex account; provide an objective summary of the text.

CCSS.ELA-LITERACY.RL.11–12.3 Analyze the impact of the author's choices regarding how to develop and relate elements of a story or drama (e.g., where a story is set, how the action is ordered, how the characters are introduced and developed).

CCSS.ELA-LITERACY.RL.11–12.4 Determine the meaning of words and phrases as they are used in the text, including figurative and connotative meanings; analyze the impact of specific word choices on meaning and tone, including words with multiple meanings or language that is particularly fresh, engaging, or beautiful. (Include Shakespeare as well as other authors.)

CCSS.ELA-LITERACY.RL.11–12.5 Analyze how an author's choices concerning how to structure specific parts of a text (e.g., the choice of where to begin or end a story, the choice to provide a comedic or tragic resolution) contribute to its overall structure and meaning as well as its aesthetic impact.

CCSS.ELA-LITERACY.RL.11–12.6 Analyze a case in which grasping a point of view requires distinguishing what is directly stated in a text from what is really meant (e.g., satire, sarcasm, irony, or understatement).

CCSS.ELA-LITERACY.RL.11–12.7 Analyze multiple interpretations of a story, drama, or poem (e.g., recorded or live production of a play or recorded novel or poetry), evaluating how each version interprets the source text.

Be Prepared
Vera Brosgol
First Second; Illustrated edition (April 24, 2018)

Image A.3 Be Prepared
From BE PREPARED by Vera Brosgol. Copyright © 2018 by Vera Brosgol. Reprinted by permission of First Second, an imprint of Roaring Brook Press, a division of Holtzbrinck Publishing Holdings Limited Partnership. All Rights Reserved.

Discussion Questions

1. React to the title, "Be Prepared". The camp uses this saying as a motto, but what does it mean? What should Vera be prepared for? Does camp actually succeed in preparing her and the other campers for different experiences in life? Explain.
2. In what ways can our cultural identity isolate us from others? When has this happened in your life? What are some of the current cultural norms associated with being an average "American"? (For Vera, it is Pizza Hut, Carvel ice cream cakes, and summer camp.)
3. Vera very much feels like an outsider, but she is not alone in feeling this way. What can you infer from Gregor or Kira's facial expressions? Did you feel sorry for them? Angry at Vera for not reaching out to them?
4. P. 168—how did her nighttime walk help Vera to realize what was important and therefore change her perspective? What is significant about the moose? How does this experience allow her final week of camp to be enjoyable?
5. Predict what will happen when the family moves to London. How might her experiences at camp help her adjust to her new home?

Brief Teaching Recommendations for Educators and Readers

1. This story is a memoir. Create a memoir based on a time in your life that taught you a meaningful lesson or when you felt left out. Draw a scene from your memoir.
2. Draw two images of yourself—one of how you see yourself and another depicting how you think others view you. Give specifics in your drawing—clothes, body language, accessories, background, etc. What makes you, you?
3. Language is a social construct. Research the significance of language. Why is it so important that the campers speak Russian while there? Do you speak a second language? Do your classmates? Do languages have the ability to bring people together? To marginalize them? Look at Vera's reaction to the speak Russian rule—why does she have difficulty following that rule at times?

4. The novel celebrates and explores the Russian Orthodox culture. While it may seem different to outsiders, it is a source of pride for Vera. Research one of the Russian symbols or stories depicted and discuss how these tales of struggle give strength to Vera and the rest of the campers.

Suggested Common Core Standards Alignment—Because they encompass the ultimate goal for reading literature in grades 9 through 12, the most relevant Common Core Standards for 11th- and 12th-grade literature are listed here.

CCSS.ELA-LITERACY.RL.11–12.1 Cite strong and thorough textual evidence to support analysis of what the text says explicitly as well as inferences drawn from the text, including determining where the text leaves matters uncertain.

CCSS.ELA-LITERACY.RL.11–12.1 Cite strong and thorough textual evidence to support analysis of what the text says explicitly as well as inferences drawn from the text, including determining where the text leaves matters uncertain.

CCSS.ELA-LITERACY.RL.11–12.3 Analyze the impact of the author's choices regarding how to develop and relate elements of a story or drama (e.g., where a story is set, how the action is ordered, how the characters are introduced and developed).

CCSS.ELA-LITERACY.RL.11–12.4 Determine the meaning of words and phrases as they are used in the text, including figurative and connotative meanings; analyze the impact of specific word choices on meaning and tone, including words with multiple meanings or language that is particularly fresh, engaging, or beautiful

CCSS.ELA-LITERACY.RL.11–12.5 Analyze how an author's choices concerning how to structure specific parts of a text (e.g., the choice of where to begin or end a story, the choice to provide a comedic or tragic resolution) contribute to its overall structure and meaning as well as its aesthetic impact.

CCSS.ELA-LITERACY.RL.11–12.6 Analyze a case in which grasping a point of view requires distinguishing what is directly stated in a text from what is really meant (e.g., satire, sarcasm, irony, or understatement).

La Voz De M.A.Y.O. Tata Rambo
Created by—Henry Barajas
Image Comics; Illustrated edition (November 12, 2019)

Vocabulary

Activist, Barrio, Dreamers, ICE, Deportation, M.A.Y.O., National Farm Workers Association, Latinx, Okinawa WWII, PTSD, migrant workers, Model Cities Program, Gentrification

People

Cesar Chavez

Dolores Huerta

Rosa Robles—2015.

Ramon Jaurigue—Tata Rambo—co-founded MAYO, helped Pascua Yaqui Tribe, WWII vet, orphan, political activist

Rey Fimbres

Congressman Udall

Don Manuel Alvarez—newsletter writer

Teddy Acuna—Newsletter editor

Rosie Jimenez—Newsletter artist

Anselmo Valencia—Yaqui Leader

Pete Lopez

Valencia

Congressman Carl Hayden

Dennis Deconcini

Questions for The Author—have students keep a running list of questions that they would want to ask the author. Some examples below:

Were you a reporter? What is your background? How did this bring you to creating a historical comic?

Can you explain your research process and comics creation—did you need to leave anything out? Would you change anything?

"This is a story about what I can prove and I think might have happened"—what parts of the comic were what you thought happened?

Ramon died before the comic came out—how do you think he would have reacted?

How did Ramon come to terms with serving during war and then dedicating his life to saving others after?

Ramon was a marine—is there more info on his experiences in WWII?

P. 11—is he adding alcohol to his coffee in the morning? Was this to deal with PTSD?

Before Reading

Pre-assess—ask students to define civil rights and give historical examples.

Have students analyze the front and back covers of the comic and predict what they will be reading about and discuss as a class.

"Over the decades, comic books by and about people of color have become an important space as corrective to an otherwise straight male, Anglo-biased historical record. . .

As Jorge Santos so aptly states, 'graphic novels and graphic memoirs present an opportunity to push against the consensus and create a more complete history.' "—from the foreword by Frederick Luis Aldama. What do these quotes mean? What other comic book/pop culture (tv, movies, music, etc.) examples are there that have helped create awareness of people outside of this narrative?

During Reading

p. 15—PREDICT—what do you think is going to happen next in this story? Why?

Why is the word "Indians" in quotation marks? What does the Congressman mean by "You're going to wake a sleeping giant?"

pp. 17–18—why would it be important for the tribe to be federally recognized?

p. 19—why would Cesar Chavez agreeing to protest with M.A.Y.O. be such an important event? (Connect with MLK coming into Selma and crossing Edmund Pettus Bridge.)

p. 21—what is the political cartoon suggesting will happen? How might people react?

p. 22—What is the reason Mr. Fimbres gives for building the highway? Is this a good enough reason?

p. 23—powerful images—do they make connections to other protests in US History? (Teacher tip—compare to images from summer of 2020, protests in the Civil Rights Movement, etc.)

p. 24—what is the meaning of the words the protestors are shouting? Why is this phrase important?

Chapter 2 Title Page—what does this term mean? Importance?

Chapter 2—shifting viewpoints to the narrator. . . .

p. 35 LGBTQIA+—what connections are there between this page and the author's own journey in creating this comic?

p. 29—too many times, we tend to put historical figures on a pedestal and think that they are perfect beings. The author chose to be completely honest about his great grandfather; how does this impact your feelings about him as an activist? Should it? What is being suggested of Jaurigue here?

p. 39—should the tribe relocate? (Perhaps this is a time to discuss the Trail of Tears, shrinking tribal lands, etc.) What options were given to the tribe? Which option do you think they should have taken? Why?

p.41—why was this such an important moment for M.A.Y.O.?

p. 41—where is Tucson? Why is it an important place for migrant workers?

p. 42—in what ways did Ramon and M.A.Y.O. try to help the community? (Connections to the Black Panthers and the breakfast program.)

p. 44—what is the impact of Ramon's activism on his family?

p. 46—substance abuse issues on reservations—small research project about reservation issues today? Why does it happen?)

pp. 50–51—reflect on the history of Native Americans, especially the Yaqui . . . What does the author mean by "They won some battles . . . but lost the war?"

p. 54—establishment of casinos—good move?

p. 54—why was M.A.Y.O. not mentioned in the tribe's history?

Chapter 3

p. 62—"People of color have fought in every war the U.S. has waged, but they're never mentioned. Specifically, Latinx will rot in the potter's field of history"—what does this mean? (This could be an opportunity for a small research project to find out what non-white males have fought/participated in U.S. wars.)

p. 62—Ramon was orphaned; do you think this played a role on why he became an activist?

p. 65—Looking at the faces of the panelists on p. 65, what do you think will be the outcome of the meeting? Why?

p. 72—Ramon's wife states that "it only cost him his home"—what does she mean by this? Do you think this was all worth it?

End—students can read through the Newsletter and primary sources to summarize the points being made.

After Reading

Refer back to the answers from the pre-assessment (in the Before Reding section) on examples of the civil rights movement. Were Latinx examples given? Why or why not? Have a discussion centering around history/historiography and how voices can often be left out. Why does this happen? How can this be corrected?

Project Ideas

p. 20—Woody Guthrie's *"This Land is Your Land"*—was this a protest song? Have students read the lyrics while listening. Ask students to share songs that they listen to that inspire making meaningful change.

Research and present on modern Native American and Latinx civil rights issues.

Research the history of the Yaqui Tribe—where are they? What about tribes in your area? What is the current state of Native Americans?

Students can research other voices that have been left out of the "textbook" and create their own comics in small groups, using tools to their comfort level. The teacher can provide a curated list of topics ahead of time or allow time for students to conduct some research on their own. Some may choose to hand draw their comics, others may use online tools such as Pixton, and some may even choose to combine different types of media into one comic. This assignment can be varied according to levels—even including a research paper, annotated works cited, etc.

What would you protest today? How would you do it? M.A.Y.O. used their newsletter, La Voz De MAYO, to spread awareness; how can it be done today? Instead of, or in addition to, the above project, students can create a modern media campaign to address modern civil rights issues. How would they do it? What tools would they use? Students can then create presentations, posters, etc., to share with the class.

Create a superhero out of one of the people in this comic. What would their superpowers be? What is their origin story? What would their hero costume look like? What other historical heroes would be on their team? What historical figures would be their arch enemies? This could be expanded to include other civil rights activists.

Students can research the impact of PTSD on soldiers, both in the past and today. What is being done to help? How can students help?

The Montgomery Story
Fellowship of Reconciliation (Author), Alfred Hassler (Author),
Benton Resnik (Author), Sy Barry (Artist)
Top Shelf Productions (November 20, 2013)
Guided Reading Packet

1. Before reading—let's predict. What do you expect to see in this comic?
2. go to https://www.learningforjustice.org/magazine/spring-2015/martin-luther-king-and-the-montgomery-story
3. Look at the front cover—now predict again. What do you expect to see/read in this comic based on the cover? Use textual evidence in your answer below. Write down one question you have/want to know more about.

Vocab

1. Jim Crow
2. Boycott
3. Nonviolence

Page 1 (page AFTER the cover)—give basic biographical information for MLK

Page 2—"I'm a peaceful man—but I have a gun"—why?

"We used to play—the baby and I—right next to the bureau with the loaded gun. I wondered if I'd have the courage to use it to defend my family. Lately, I've started to wonder if that really would be courage"—what is Jones talking about? What does he think real courage is? (Infer.)

Page 3—what's the plan to support Rosa Parks?

Page 4—Montgomery Improvement Association—what does MLK mean by "walk to freedom"?

Page 5— what was the solution to not having a bus to ride?

What was the role of the police during the boycott? Why?

Page 6—what happened in MLK's home?

The crowd was ready to enact revenge—why was this not carried out?

Page 7—why did the protest leaders turn themselves in?

Why did they role-play what to do when allowed back on the bus?

Page 8—what was the ruling of the supreme court?

Top of page, second panel—describe the look of Jones getting on the bus—how is this an example of nonviolence? Is this successful?

Bottom of page—last panel—foreshadowing—what is going to happen next?

Page 9—Reverend Robert Graetz—what was his role? What makes him stand out in this story?

Page 10—what happened in India? How did Gandhi's methods compare to MLK's?

Page 11—how was Gandhi able to be successful in his struggle against the British? Compare to MLK.

Pages 12–14—bullet the major tenets of the Montgomery Method.

Explain the middle panel on page 12—what is the significance of the mirror?

Go back and reread. How would you summarize/explain this method to someone? Evaluate it—successful?

Why do you think this comic book was made?

Name: Class: Date:

March: Book One
by John Lewis (Author), Andrew Aydin (Author),
Nate Powell (Illustrator)
Top Shelf Productions; Illustrated edition (March 22, 2016)
Guided Reading Packet

1. Why do you think this book is titled—*March*?

Opening—Do NOT read ahead. (Photocopy first three pages to keep from reading ahead?)

1. Pages 5–7—what is happening in this scene? Why might those walking across the bridge be concerned about swimming? Describe the two sides in this event. What is going to happen to the man in the backpack?
2. **Small research project**—at your tables, find out what happened. Write a description below—who are the people involved, what happened, why did it happen, etc. Be sure to include your credible source information.
3. After completing your research, draw a sketch of what your group thinks will happen next on page 8. We will share with the class.
4. Pages 12–15—what is the significance of the date? What happened? Where is this person going? Who do you think he is? How do you think he would feel about this event? Why?
5. Pages 16–17—where is this? This is the same man from #4—who is he? How do you know? Where is he?
6. Pages 18–20—why does the mother want her children to visit his office? Who are "we"? What does Mr. Lewis tell the family he did on Aug 28th, 1963? (We will listen to what he said.)
7. If you could meet any person of historical importance—just walk into his/her office—who would it be and why? (Does not have to still be living.)
8. Pages 20–35—Mr. Lewis' background. Give a short bio below. How would this inspire him to become a civil rights leader? Pay attention to the way he treated the chickens—how would this foreshadow his later work? What is the connection?
9. Page 35—". . . but school wasn't important to me, and it was ultimately the **reason** I got involved in the Civil Rights Movement"—predict—why?

10. Pages 36–47—June 1951—a trip north. Why did they not stop at restaurants until they were out of the South? React to this information—how does it make you feel?
    Why would African-Americans travelling into the South from the North face potentially greater issues?
    – In what state did they finally feel a bit safer?
    – Page 43—"I couldn't believe it—they had WHITE people living next door to them"—react.
    – Page 47—"After that trip, home never felt the same. And neither did I"—why? What would be the impact on Mr. Lewis?
11. Pages 48–52—detail the differences in the lives of whites and blacks—give specific textual evidence. Describe the efforts Mr. Lewis took to attend school.
12. Page 53—Brown VS the Board of Education of Topeka—quick research—what was the issue and outcome of this case?
13. Pages 55–56—what was the impact of hearing MLK speak on the radio? Why?
14. Page 56—was everything going to work with desegregation? Explain.
15. August, 1957—Emmett Till—why was he killed? What happened at the trial? Your reaction. . .
16. Page 58 Rosa Parks—what happened? Why? What was the boycott to accomplish?
17. Pages 59–60—what inspired John Lewis to become a preacher? Why?
18. Pages 64–65—where did Mr. Lewis apply to college? Why?
19. Page 66—Troy State—what was the issue? Why was Mr. Lewis turned away? Who did he turn to for help? With whom did he meet?
20. Pages 68–71—First meeting with MLK. How did John Lewis feel? Evidence? What was the plan for Troy State? Potential repercussions? Would **YOU** do it? Why or why not?
21. Pages 72–73—Did Mr. Lewis decide to sue Troy State? Why or why not?
22. Page 75—Non-violence. Why did the Black Baptists leave the other church?
    – Look up Jim Lawson and Diane Nash—give a 3–4 sentence bio for each.
23. Page 77—What was discussed at the meeting?—how would these issues be solved—through what method?
24. Pages 79–83—Why would they call each other such horrible names? How would this prepare them? Give specific textual evidence. How would **YOU** react?

25. What was the first target for their non-violent resistance? Why?
26. Pages 84–86—How would they initially find out what stores to target? How did they initially protest? Why were the white students refused service? Your thoughts?
27. Pages 87–91—Woolworth's—describe the feelings of the people—use textual evidence.
28. Pages 92–93—what did the employees do in response?
29. Pages 94–97—was the sit-in a success? This is your opinion—use textual evidence.
30. Page 98—Feb 1960—number of protestors grow with each success. Will Campbell—white minister—why was he "run out of Mississippi"?
31. Page 99—What happened differently at this protest?
32. Page 100—"Violence does beget violence. But the opposite is just as true"—meaning?
33. Page 101—why did the counter-protestors stop?
34. Page 102—what were the actions of the police?
35. Pages 103–105—did the arrests stop the protests?
36. Page 106—role of each of the following:
    Dr. Stephen J. Wright
    – Z. Alexander Looby
    – Thurgood Marshall
37. Page 107—how will the trial turn out? Will the students be found guilty or innocent? How do you know? Use evidence from the drawing.
38. Page 108—"Jail, no bail"—explain. Why do they want to take this tactic?
39. Page 109—the students were forced to do manual labor as punishment—how did others in America react? Why was Jim Lawson released?
40. Page 110—TN Governor Buford Ellington—why was he upset about the protests? What two things were done to increase the protesting?
41. Page 111—were these new protests effective? Why did Mr. Lewis disagree with Thurgood Marshall?
42. Page 112—Give a brief summary of the below groups—goals, etc.
    SCLC
    – **NAACP**
    – **SNCC**
43. Page 116—phone rings—Looby's house was bombed—why? What is the response?

44. Page 117—PREDICT—based on what you have already read—what do you think is going to happen next?
45. Pages 118–119—what is your opinion of Mayor West? Why?
46. Page 120—MLK arrived to speak. On May 10, 1960—Nashville stores agreed to do what?
47. Page 121—is everything now "ok" in Nashville? Give textual evidence.
48. This graphic novel is part of a trilogy—what do you think will happen in books two and three?
49. The Spirit of History was mentioned several times in the book—what do you think this means?
50. Give a quick response to having read this graphic novel.

Name: Date:

Guided Reading for *March Book 2*
by John Lewis (Author), Andrew Aydin (Author),
Nate Powell (Illustrator)
Top Shelf Productions; Illustrated edition (January 20, 2015)

For Book 2, I amass a large collection of different sized/colored sticky notes and leave a bunch on each table in the classroom. Students read the book with sticky notes in hand and just place them in the book whenever they feel moved. They can put in a note for a vital part of the story, a question, a personal or historical connection, a panel they want to share, etc. They are also asked to write some comments on multiple notes in the book to explain their choice of panel or page. Initially, I thought I'd have to give a minimum amount of notes to include. However, the first time we did this lesson, I just let the students decide on when to react, and it was powerful to see books overflowing with sticky notes.

Before the end of each reading class day, we leave time to share in the large group, and students will often share specific panels with the class and their powerful reactions. I go through each book at the end of the lesson and create a summary reaction for each student as I take out the sticky notes. Some of the reactions are simply exclamation points and question marks. Others are multiple sticky notes piled on top of one another as the student wrote a detailed reaction. As a teacher, this idea was scary at first—the idea of just letting go and not holding students accountable for each and every page of reading. I learned that this authentic reading experience moved the students to share with one another even more often as they felt empowered.

March Book III
by John Lewis (Author), Andrew Aydin (Author),
Nate Powell (Illustrator)
Top Shelf Productions; Illustrated edition (August 2, 2016)

1. **Pages 4–25 (end on the title page that says March: Book Three)**
   A. Summarize what you saw on these pages (use specific examples).
   B. One question you have.
   C. One reaction to something specific—give a page number and describe the panel and your reaction.
2. **Pages 26–42**
   A. Summarize what you saw on these pages (use specific examples).
   B. One question you have.
   C. One reaction to something specific—give a page number and describe the panel and your reaction.
3. **Pages 43–73**
   A. Summarize what you saw on these pages (use specific examples).
   B. One question you have.
   C. One reaction to something specific—give a page number and describe the panel and your reaction.
4. **Pages 74–95**
   A. Summarize what you saw on these pages (use specific examples).
   B. One question you have.
   C. One reaction to something specific—give a page number and describe the panel and your reaction.
5. **Pages 96–117**
   A. Summarize what you saw on these pages (use specific examples).
   B. One question you have.
   C. One reaction to something specific—give a page number and describe the panel and your reaction.
6. **Pages 118–145**
   A. Summarize what you saw on these pages (use specific examples).
   B. One question you have.
   C. One reaction to something specific—give a page number and describe the panel and your reaction.

7. **Pages 146–169**
   A. Summarize what you saw on these pages (use specific examples).
   B. One question you have.
   C. One reaction to something specific—give a page number and describe the panel and your reaction.
8. **Pages 170–191**
   A. Summarize what you saw on these pages (use specific examples).
   B. One question you have.
   C. One reaction to something specific—give a page number and describe the panel and your reaction.
9. **Pages 192–218**
   A. Summarize what you saw on these pages (use specific examples).
   B. One question you have.
   C. One reaction to something specific—give a page number and describe the panel and your reaction.
10. **Pages 219–246**
   A. Summarize what you saw on these pages (use specific examples).
   B. One question you have.
   C. One reaction to something specific—give a page number and describe the panel and your reaction.

Culminating project after reading March -

Create a comic book based on a modern civil rights issue. Students will be placed into small groups, choose a modern issue, research, and create the comic. Students can either draw it by hand or use an online tool, such as Pixton. Often, students will choose an artist in the group to create the comic cover and then use Pixton to create the actual comic inside. Each group will choose a different topic than the others (e.g., LGTBQ+, Latino, education disparities, physical/mental disability, women's rights, etc.). The comic must contain statistics and examples of the civil rights violations for credible sources and include an annotated works cited page.

After we have finished reading all three March graphic novels, I ask students to define the term "civil rights" and agree to a common definition as a class. I then ask them to brainstorm and to come up with at least five current civil rights issues. We share these issues as a class and give a brief explanation of how these issues match with the class definition of "civil rights".

Students then decide which issue they would like to further research and to create an original comic about. Students are welcome to undertake this project as an individual, in pairs, or as a small group. I ask the small groups to explain to me how each student will be individually involved in the project and why it will take multiple students to complete. I can adjust my expectations for each group and individual as needed.

Comic Requirements:

Minimum of six pages.
Must have SPECIFIC information/data included on each page—think quotes, surveys, census, etc.
Each page must have at least five panels (if you are creating an important splash page, this requirement can be waved).
Can be hand drawn, use Pixton, or a combination of both (example—hand draw the covers and use Pixton for the interior).
Must have an awesome cover and title that catch the eye of the reader.
The civil rights issue must be clear—include a brief summary of the nature of your chosen topic.
This is not to be a retelling of an event, but rather your (or your group's) fictional account incorporating specific credible data. The comic needs to be a complete story—think intro, climax, resolution. What is your realistic solution to the issue?
Annotated Works Cited Page with a minimum of five sources—you

need to include a summary of information found with each source and an explanation of the credibility of this source.

Before beginning the creation of the original comic, students must present a storyboard with sketches of what they will be creating. This allows me, as the teacher, to make sure students don't waste time and become frustrated when hitting dead ends in research or solution to their chosen issue. It is vital to continually check in with each group or individual throughout the creation process. I also give a PowerPoint presentation of comics that focus on civil rights issues (many already mentioned in this book) and give time for the students to look through the comics to gain inspiration.

When the work is complete, we upload the comics and share them with one another. As we present and discuss, students always remark on the connectedness between these issues and even in possible solutions. As a class, we bring together real-world solutions to these issues, and the students feel empowered. They were able to research and create an original story to become personally and emotionally involved in the plight of people who just want to be treated with respect and equality. They know how they can become involved, even without the right to vote. They understand their role and responsibility in a greater society.

The Amazing Spider-Man #36

Resource: Spider-Man Vol. 2 #36, December 2001. This comic can be purchased online (often around $50) or through Comixology.com (also through Amazon) online for $1.99. (Also—no better resource than https://www.911memorial.org/museum.)

Purpose: What happens in the world is reflected in pop culture—in literature (e.g., Frankenstein and the Industrial Revolution), music, movies, plays, TV shows, movies, etc. In this instance, Spider-Man #36 was published following the events of 9/11/01 and showcases much of the feelings felt in the weeks and months following the attacks. As such, comics can serve as societal artifacts and can be evaluated as such in the classroom. Students will read this comic as a window into 9/11 and discuss what it can tell us about the American society into which it was published.

(Note—this comic does not have page numbers. I began counting with the first page being the one with the GPS coordinates, and I continued counting every page after—including pages with advertisements in my count.)

Before Reading/Do Now I would suggest a discussion about 9/11—causes and effects—before beginning this lesson.

Part I

1. Can comic books be used in the classroom as artifacts? Why or why not?
2. Pair/share with a partner and then discuss as a class.

Part II

3. Bibliographic information—cite this comic in MLA format. (Tip—date is on the first page, author/illustrator info is on the last page.)
4. Flip to the inside title page. When was this comic published? Why is this important to note?
5. Predict—what do you think you will read about in this comic?

Part III

6. Turn to page 1. Using Google Maps, find the GPS coordinates given. Switch to satellite view and explore the area. What is the connection between this location and the date of the comic? (This would be a good time to discuss latitude and longitude, GPS satellites, etc.)

During Reading:

7. Turn to pages 2 and 3. What is Spider-Man seeing? What happened? Go back to your answer for #6 and use the Google Maps image to determine what Spider-Man is seeing. Write down how this image makes you feel. (Teachers—this is when I show images of Ground Zero—especially the images of the wreckage as this is seen throughout the comic. Students can then draw an arrow from where Spider-Man is located and where the Twin Towers were located.)

8. Compare the illustrated images of Ground Zero to those taken that day. Compare and contrast these images—write down your thoughts.

9. Page 4—What are the civilians conveying to Spider-Man? In what way do you think this matched the feelings of many Americans? (Students can read and discuss the 1993 attack on the World Trade Center—https://www.cnn.com/2013/11/05/us/1993-world-trade-center-bombing-fast-facts/index.html.)

10. On page 6, Spider-Man calls the attackers "madmen". Do you think this is accurate? Were the attackers insane? Why do you think these people chose to conduct this attack?

11. Look closely at the ruble on pages 6 and 7—what/who do you notice in the wreckage?

12. Page 12—Analyze the narrator's words (Spider-Man) and compare to the images. What is the significance of the poses and facial features on the characters?

13. Page 14—Who are the true heroes of whom Spider-Man is talking? (There are multiple powerful images of the destruction done to first responder vehicles available to use as comparison to those drawn in the comic.)

14. Page 15—panels 4 and 5—What event is being depicted?

15. Page 16, panels 1–3—List the reasons Spider-Man is discussing as to why the United States was attacked.

16. Page 16, panel 4—"bodies in freefall on the evening news"—what happened?

17. Page 16, panel 5—Describe the different feelings in the two different groups being portrayed in this panel. Using specific visual evidence, where are they? What is the connection to "crusades of the past"?

18. Page 19, panel 1—"that the most harmed are the least deserving"—to whom is Spider-Man referring?

19. Page 19—Who is the little boy's father? What happened to him? Use specific visual evidence in your answer.

20. Page 20—Spider-Man discusses "the death of innocence". What does he mean? Do you think the United States was truly "innocent"?
21. Page 20 "Rage compounded upon rage. Rage enough to blot out the sun." What does Spider-Man mean? As many Americans were angry, what response did the United States government give to these events in the months following the attacks?
22. Page 22—So many are asking "why" as to the causes of the attacks. Why do you think they happened?
23. Page 24—Describe the feelings of Captain America using specific visual evidence. Compare the feelings of Americans to those of Captain America—what is the symbolism of using this specific character?
24. Page 25 panel 1—Spider-Man says, "Do we tell them evil is a foreign face?" Do some people think in this manner? Can the visualization of "terrorism" in media be portrayed as a "Middle Eastern" or "Muslim" face? Why?
25. Page 26—Again, Spider-Man states that no one could stop it or see it coming. Do you think this is true? (I discuss the Crusades, Inquisition, Sykes-Picot Agreement, and other historical interactions between the "West" and "Middle East". How does history affect 9/11? We can analyze these events as "excuses" or "reasons".)
26. Page 26—What is the United States military planning on doing in response? How does Spider-Man feel about this action? Respond with specific textual and visual evidence.
27. Pages 27, 30, 31, and 32—How does Spider-Man feel Americans should respond?
28. Pages 27, 30, 31, and 32—What is the significance of those who are drawn in these panels? What is the artist conveying about America?

After Reading Part III

29. Reflect on this comic as a whole—how would you describe it to someone in 5 sentences?
30. Do you think this comic is useful as an artifact for use in the classroom? Explain.
31. What do you wish the artist/author would have done differently? Added in? Taken out?
32. What questions do you have? What would you ask the author or illustrator?
33. Why do you think Marvel chose to publish this comic?
34. What panel was the most impactful to you? Why?

Part IV—Pair/share and then whole-class discussion.

Part V—Possible extension activities.

1. Students can then go back and analyze the comic as a physical artifact, ignoring the story. What can the advertisements tell us about the time period? What is being sold? What are the prices? Are students surprised that there are advertisements in this type of comic? (Page 25, last panel, discusses Gameboys and VCRs.)

2. Students can create a PowerPoint presentation showing historical photographs they find that might have inspired the artist.

3. Students can create their own comics about 9/11 or other historical events. Ask them what event has been most impactful in their lives, of the history of America or the world. Students could combine in small groups to make this comic—it can be a combination of hand drawn and computer tools. Often, artists in the group decide to draw the front and back covers, while the rest of the group uses online tools to create the pages inside.

Name: Date:

Star Wars—Point of View
Star Wars (2015) #21 Marvel Comics
Jason Aaron writer, Jorge Molina penciller, David Aja cover artist

I.   BEFORE opening the comic book, answer question #1.

1. **Are Stormtroopers good or evil? Explain and provide several examples—no wrong answer. If you are stuck, it is ok to ask a partner.**
2. As you read, pick out **specific textual evidence** to reexamine the original prompt—are Stormtroopers good or evil? You will summarize what is going on for each page number—look at both images and text. Think—is this page about Storm-troopers being good or evil? At the end of reading the comic, you will be writing an open-ended response to answer this question using the evidence from the comic book.

Do not leave any page blank except for advertisements.

Page 1—example—the empire wants to eliminate the rebels. Elite stormtroopers will be hunting them down. Sounds evil to me.
Page 2—example—someone on the ship is telling how his father was murdered in front of him—now he/she was going to be killing. Sounds evil to me!
Page 3
Page 4
Page 5—Advertisement—skip
Page 6
Page 7
Page 8 Advertisement—skip
Page 9
Page 10
Page 11
Page 12
Page 13
Page 14
Page 15
Page 16

II. Using all of the above information, you will be writing an essay
to answer the following prompt: As presented in this comic, **are
Stormtroopers good or evil?** Pick a side.

Name: Date:

Comics as Artifacts Part 1

1. What is a historical artifact? What are some examples?

2. How can historians use these artifacts to tell us about civilizations?

Name: Date:

Comics as Artifacts Part 2

1. If you have a favorite superhero, comic series, or graphic novel, please list below

2. Overall, what is your opinion of comic books? Why?

3. As a class of historians, is it acceptable to use comic books as historical artifacts? In other words, can we learn about social studies through these sources? Explain why or why not—be sure to include specific examples (we can learn about _____ by reading comic books. We cannot learn about history through comic books because _____).

Name: Date:

Comics as Artifacts Part III

1. Title of Comic:

2. Author and Illustrator:

3. Publishing Company:

4. Copyright Date:

5. Let's assume that a reader can learn a lot about a society by reading its comic books. What can your comic tell you about the society in which it was published? Bullet SPECIFIC examples from the comic to showcase your findings.

Name: Date:

Comics as Artifacts Part IV

Directions: when you have finished critically analyzing your comic book, pair/share your information with a partner. Answer the questions below.

1. Name of partner:

2. What is your partner's opinion about comic books?

3. What information did he/she give you about the comic book that helped you analyze the society? Did your partner give you any new insight into how to analyze your comic book?

4. What do you and your partner think about using comic books as historical resources? Explain.

Name: Date:

Nat Turner by Kyle Baker
Abrams ComicArts; Illustrated edition (June 1, 2008)

Read the introduction and answer the following questions:

1. Who was Nat Turner?

2. What did he do?

3. How did he do it? (What was his superpower?)

4. What are your thoughts about Turner and what you are about to read?

5. Why is it important that we learn about Nat Turner?

Name: Date:

Nat Turner by Kyle Baker

Directions: As you read through the first 56 pages of the graphic novel, write down your reactions/thoughts/questions. What is happening on each page? It is ok to take a guess, as long as you have specific evidence to back up your observation. (Each portion of the reaction sheet represents two pages in the book.)

Pages 1 and 2
Pages 3 and 4
Pages 5 and 6
Pages 7 and 8
Pages 9 and 10
Pages 11 and 12
Pages 13 and 14
Pages 15 and 16
Pages 17 and 18
Pages 19 and 20
Pages 21 and 22
Pages 23 and 24
Pages 25 and 26
Pages 27 and 28
Pages 29 and 30
Pages 31 and 32
Pages 33 and 34
Pages 35 and 36
Pages 37 and 38
Pages 39 and 40
Pages 41 and 42
Pages 43 and 44
Pages 45 and 46
Pages 47 and 48
Pages 49 and 50
Pages 51 and 52
Pages 53 and 54
Pages 55 and 56

Reaction—what is your overall reaction to this reading selection? What have you learned?

Finally—draw what you think happens next. It could be in the next hour, next week, next month, or as far into the future as you want. You can draw an image or create a short comic of your own.

Name: Date:

**The Great War: July 1, 1916: The First Day of the Battle
of the Somme by Joe Sacco
W. W. Norton & Company; Illustrated edition (November 4, 2013)**

Directions: You will walk along the laid-out comic tapestry to complete this sheet. There are no wrong answers as long as you provide specific textual evidence to back up your observations. There are 24 plates/sections in the tapestry, and your job is to react to at least twelve, asking questions and giving reactions. When you are finished, write down two overall questions you have and also give a short summation of your reaction/what you have learned. We will then have a chance to share our findings and questions in small group and then in large group discussions. Finally, we will look at the author's annotations and compare them to our responses. When looking at the tapestry, be sure to make a note of the one plate that stuck out the most to you.

Plate 1
Plate 2
Plate 3
Plate 4
Plate 5
Plate 6
Plate 7
Plate 8
Plate 9
Plate 10
Plate 11
Plate 12
Plate 13
Plate 14
Plate 15
Plate 16
Plate 17
Plate 18
Plate 19
Plate 20
Plate 21
Plate 22

Plate 23
Plate 24

Two overall questions:
Overall opinion/what you have learned:
Plate that stuck out to you the most and why:

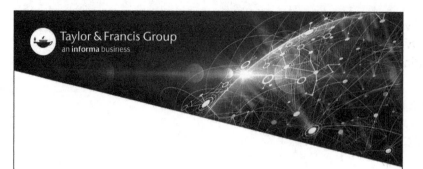